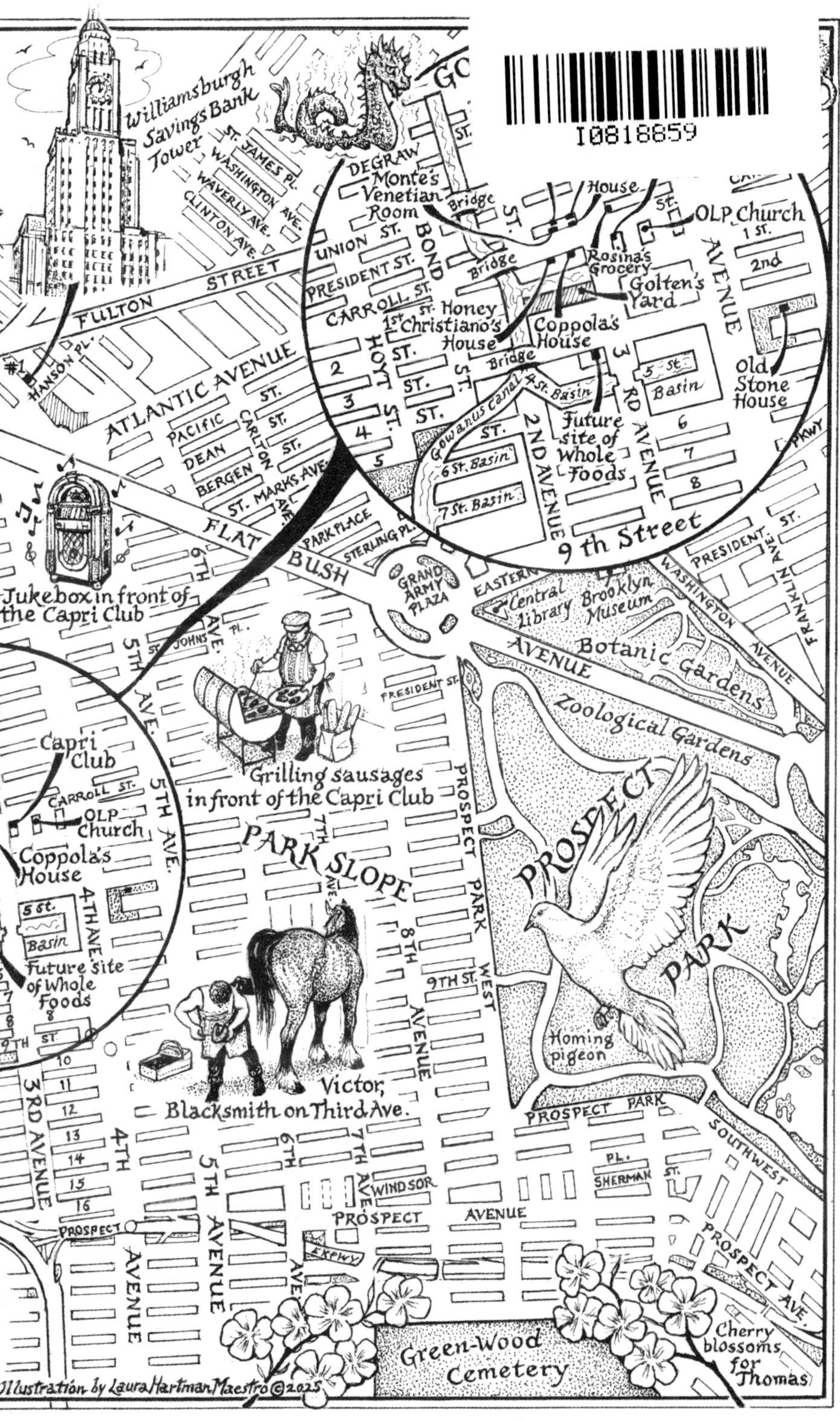
I0818859
Williamsburgh Savings Bank Tower
ST. JAMES PL.
WASHINGTON AVE.
WAVERLY AVE.
CLINTON AVE.
DEGRAW
Monte's Venetian Room
Bridge
UNION ST.
PRESIDENT ST.
CARROLL ST.
BOND
1st ST.
Honey Christiano's House
Bridge
Rosina's Grocery
Golten's Yard
Coppola's House
OLP Church
1 ST.
2nd
AVENUE
Old Stone House
HOYT ST.
2 ST.
3 ST.
4 ST.
5
Gowanus Canal
4 St. Basin
5 St. Basin
6 St. Basin
7 St. Basin
2ND AVENUE
3RD AVENUE
Future site of Whole Foods
6
7
8
9 th Street
PKWY
FULTON STREET
HANSON PL.
#1
ATLANTIC AVENUE
PACIFIC ST.
DEAN ST.
BERGEN ST.
CARLTON AVE.
ST. MARKS AVE.
FLATBUSH
PARK PLACE
STERLING PL.
GRAND ARMY PLAZA
EASTERN
Central Library
Brooklyn Museum
PRESIDENT ST.
WASHINGTON AVENUE
FRANKLIN AVE.
Jukebox in front of the Capri Club
6TH AVE.
ST. JOHNS PL.
5TH AVE.
Botanic Gardens
Zoological Gardens
Capri Club
CARROLL ST.
OLP Church
Coppola's House
4TH AVE.
5 St. Basin
Future site of Whole Foods
9TH ST.
Grilling sausages in front of the Capri Club
PRESIDENT ST.
PROSPECT PARK WEST
PARK SLOPE
7TH AVE.
8TH AVENUE
9TH ST.
PROSPECT PARK
Homing pigeon
Victor, Blacksmith on Third Ave.
10
11
12
13
14
15
16
3RD AVENUE
4TH AVENUE
5TH AVENUE
6TH AVE.
7TH AVE.
WINDSOR
PROSPECT PARK SOUTHWEST
PL.
SHERMAN ST.
PROSPECT AVENUE
PROSPECT
EXPWY
PROSPECT AVE.
Green-Wood Cemetery
Cherry blossoms for Thomas
Illustration by Laura Hartman Maestro © 2025

GOWANUS CROSSING

GOWANUS CROSSING

A Brooklyn Boyhood

VINCENT COPPOLA

Henry Holt and Company
New York

Henry Holt and Company
Publishers since 1866
120 Broadway
New York, New York 10271
www.henryholt.com

Henry Holt® and Ⓗ® are registered trademarks of Macmillan Publishing Group, LLC.
EU Representative: Macmillan Publishers Ireland Ltd., 1st Floor, The Liffey Trust Centre, 117–126 Sheriff Street Upper, Dublin 1, D01 YC43

Distributed in Canada by Raincoast Book Distribution Limited

Library of Congress Cataloging-in-Publication Data

Names: Coppola, Vincent, author.
Title: Gowanus crossing : a Brooklyn boyhood / Vincent Coppola.
Description: First edition. | New York : Henry Holt and Company, 2026.
Identifiers: LCCN 2025040602 | ISBN 9781250904126 (hardcover) | ISBN 9781250904119 (ebook)
Subjects: LCSH: Coppola, Vincent—Childhood and youth | Italian Americans—New York (State)—New York—Biography | Journalists—United States—Biography | Brooklyn (New York, N.Y.)—Biography | LCGFT: Autobiographies
Classification: LCC F129.B7 C76 2026 | DDC 974.7/2300451—dc23/eng/20260203
LC record available at https://lccn.loc.gov/2025040602

First Edition 2026

Designed by Meryl Sussman Levavi

Printed in the United States of America

10 9 8 7 6 5 4 3 2 1

For Suzanne

Contents

GOWANUS CROSSING

Prologue

Brooklyn is a mythic place. Gowanus is its Nile, pestilent and fertile, forever reborn and reimagined. Mother to motherless Brooklyn's wanderers, poets, misfits, dreamers, junkies, and schemers, to the immigrant poor landed on its fatal shores.

When I was growing up, no one would have mistaken the Gowanus for the Nile or any other living body of water. It was an open sewer, stagnant, reeking, sluggish, meandering from Butler Street—today's Boerum Hill—through a graveyard of decayed nineteenth-century industrial plants, abandoned warehouses, dying marine repair facilities, rotting docks, its future already past. I played pirates on half-sunken barges, sought treasure among barrels of glittering industrial chemicals, climbed ladders and through hatches of gigantic rusted marine diesel engines. I watched boats leaking fuel oil churn through the canal, crews desperate to escape the stench. And sometimes, in the lot behind the John P. Carlson ink factory, I glimpsed men dumping medical waste and other unmentionable things into the glistening green water.

Gowanus was poisoned but forever fertile: a salt marsh known to Dutch settlers who exported its succulent oysters to Amsterdam; the scene of a disastrous Revolutionary War battle fought three blocks from my house, unknown to me except in neighborhood stories that somehow managed to conflate George Washington and George Patton. The canal I knew was filtered through *Huckleberry Finn, The Time Machine, Treasure Island.* Over time, I left it behind like Coney Island and Steeplechase Park. Or so I thought. I'm an old man now, and Gowanus is a Superfund site in the midst of a real estate boom, once slippery banks blooming with million-dollar condominiums. The abandoned rat-infested powerhouse where Americo Guzzi inadvertently cracked my head with a paint-dripping lead pipe—he had a notoriously bad throwing arm—is somehow an arts center.

✦ ✦ ✦

My family arrived on the Gowanus in the 1890s, along with our priests, merchants, malefactors, culture, traditions, and animosities, lifted intact from the impoverished towns and villages south of Naples. A new world rose among the canal's ruins—fish markets, *salumerie,* butcher shops, the pastry store where Sinatra "always" bought *sfogliatella,* ten-cent pizza, three-dollar gallons of homemade wine, murder, bookie joints, crones out of fairy tales selling calzones and lemon ice. On Nevins Street, Mohawk ironworkers packed the Wigwam bar; on Carroll Street, my street, a curly-haired peddler named Angioletti sang the names of fruits and vegetables in Italian, clopping along in a horse and wagon. On Third

Avenue, a blacksmith in a leather vest worked his forge like Vulcan, sending sparks and the aromas of molten steel, smoldering hooves, and combusting coal swirling into the air. A rooster who'd lost track of time crowed at all hours. Nuns in swirling habits chased me and my friends as we clung to the back of the B37 bus. Stickball games, crap games, card games, street corner gamblers handicapping Aqueduct or Belmont. And yards from the canal, Monte's Venetian Room, our equator.

A *Through the Looking-Glass* world where everyone was loud, crude, histrionic, larger-than-life, hurtling headlong toward some disaster but at the same time fiercely loyal, compassionate, and hilariously funny. From our tar paper roof, I stared at the towers of the "city," Manhattan, unreachable as Oz but just a few subway stops away.

My parents never finished high school. Neither did my friends. This wasn't poverty—though I often went to class with cardboard stuffed in my shoes—so much as the afterbirth of a cynical, inward-looking peasant culture. A man earned a living with his hands, sometimes his fists, but rarely his mind. Joe, my father, labored in the holds of ships, in the grip of a corrupt Mafia-controlled union. He died in his sixties. As did Gloria, my mother, the sexiest woman in Gowanus. At Joe's funeral, a Sicilian, old beyond his years, whispered, "Your father, he was an *animale.*"

Correct on so many levels.

✦ ✦ ✦

Time passed. I graduated from Brooklyn College, taught in the same Williamsburg vocational high school that expelled my father. From my classroom windows, I could see Manhattan's towers across the East River, still seemingly unreachable. A Swedish woman I'd met on my first trip out of the country told me about this journalism school at Columbia University.

I applied and, somehow, was accepted.

✦ ✦ ✦

Autumn 1976. On a clear, crisp Sunday morning, when even Gowanus is hushed and beautiful. Church bells toll; the aroma of simmering tomato sauce wafts from a dozen houses. I stand on Third Avenue outside Tony's Barbershop with some older guys with nicknames like Muzzi, Funzi, Blubberhead, waiting for the Giants' kickoff. The talk is, as always, of bets and odds and the terrible Giants quarterback.

I spot a solitary biker meandering across the canal. As he approaches, I notice he's wearing tight spandex shorts and a colorful racing jersey. Bearded, helmeted, riding a skinny Italian racer, obviously from another planet. The Italian guys I'm with sport canary-yellow and baby-blue leisure suits, heavy gold chains. Passing us, the biker nods politely and pedals on toward Prospect Park. No one says a word. How could we know we were staring at the future?

In the millennium, the trickle of artists and musicians seeking edgy, affordable space for loft living, studios, agencies, and galleries becomes a moneyed flood driving up rents and property values. My neighbors, unable to afford the houses we grew up in, leave for Staten Island and Jersey. A handful, strangers in their own land, remain behind. The hip newcomers dub us "originals," but I miss the joke.

Restaurants, bars, health clubs, coffee shops, dance studios, and music venues proliferate. Andrew Pontone's casket company becomes, with no hint of irony, the Royal

Palms Shuffleboard Club. Monte's, a destination for politicians, lawyers, gangsters, entertainers, schemers for a century, reopens as a Japanese tapas bar.

I thought I'd left it all behind, but inexorably, I'm caught in the canal's tidal pull.

✦ ✦ ✦

The jetliner floats across the Narrows. Now in my seventies, I find myself pressed against the porthole, straining to pick out childhood Brooklyn landmarks—the Verrazano Bridge, Green-Wood Cemetery, Prospect Park, my school, parish church, and briefly, the glint of sunlight on green water, the Gowanus. Unbidden, memories float up from the miasma: lying under my grandfather's persimmon tree, tracing airplanes overhead with my finger; July Fourth backyard barbecues, my father happily feeding dozens of guests; him shaking a heavy fist at the heavens, demanding to know why God is killing his beautiful son Thomas.

Gloria, Joe, and Thomas are long gone, my friends and family vanished, mortality in the air like early frost. Yet, in Gowanus, the ground, the air, the water pulsing in the canal are transforming. Life, throbbing and vital, being reanimated.

I've been away forty years working in the South as a reporter, then a ghostwriter immersed in other people's lives but adrift in my own. When cancer comes calling, as it has for so many of us in Gowanus, I'm not surprised.

Surviving is the surprise.

My life has taken root in Savannah, Georgia, among nineteenth-century row houses, cobblestone streets, parochial schools, pealing church bells, the occasional scent of ocean so much like downtown Brooklyn, it's painful. There, an unlovely Gothic tower has displaced the familiar Williamsburgh Savings Bank—I marked my life by the crawl of its gargantuan clock—as Brooklyn's tallest building. On Third Avenue, Chitty's fruit stand has disappeared. Next door, the shadowed Capri Club, a Mafia redoubt, is somehow Baba's Pierogies. Our family house, brick facade once bulging with middle-age spread, has been reengineered into an edgy blue-brick town house, an insouciant spray of bamboo out front. When I peer through the dusty glass of what had been Monte's Venetian Room, Gowanus's timeless characters, Honey Christiano, Sonny the Indian in his black leather trench coat, my star-crossed aunt Lucy, come alive.

I stop at Our Lady of Peace's World War II memorial, run my fingers across my father's name just as I did as a child. Two thousand names engraved in bronze, a hundred KIA, all from one struggling Italian parish. My cousin Anthony Pepe who died at Pearl Harbor is among them. A millennial appears alongside me, photographs the names with his iPhone. For what possible reason? I want to resent him, but it strikes me, he too, like the guys now kayaking on the Gowanus, is being pulled into the Gowanus Canal's timeless current.

As am I.

CHAPTER ONE

A Battered Heart

I was thirteen when I wrote "A Battered War Helmet." The assignment: bring an inanimate object to life and create its history. Sister Mary Malachy called it "a personified autobiography," a phrase from a world far beyond the Gowanus Canal.

I spend my afternoons working on it on the scarred kitchen table of our three-room apartment above a candy store, ignoring the squeals of my brothers, the blare of the Mouseketeers on channel 7, praying I can avoid one of my father's violent squalls which flicker like heat lightning in the corners of our lives. I write in ballpoint on loose-leaf paper, inspired by a movie, *Sands of Iwo Jima.* I polish it so many times, I choke up when I read it.

I hand it in and await Malachy's response.

And wait some more.

Waiting defined life in those days. Hours ticking slowly from the first bell to lunch hour; the rosary recited aloud each morning; me trying to remember its confounding mysteries; the long lines in the schoolyard and me hoping just to brush Jean W's arm as we make our way back to the classroom; the interminable church services; the nuns, black-robed prison guards, checking off attendance rolls; my frayed shirt collar stiff with starch rubbing against my neck. Vast deserts of time never to be reclaimed.

And me, thirsting for experience. At thirteen, I still believe in the cascading prayers we recite each morning, in the "forgiveness of sins, the resurrection of the body, life everlasting." Part of me longs, in the words of a song my mother sang to me when I was a little boy, to be a "stout-hearted man."

From my assigned seat in the back of the class surrounded by dunces and troublemakers, I wait for Malachy to appear with her brass-buckled black leather schoolbag, eager for the telltale bulge of marked papers. One morning, it's there. Time crawls. It's almost lunchtime when Malachy reaches into the bag and pulls out the sheaf of papers. I smirk at the chicken pox smear across the title page. Someone else's essay.

"I have your papers," she begins. "Some of you worked hard and turned in excellent papers. The rest, the *vulgarians*"—she looks up balefully—"handed in stuff and nonsense. You know who you are."

I sit on the edge of my seat. She hands out the A papers. "Cireno, Cucciaro, D'Alessio, DiLorenzo . . ."

What about Coppo . . . ?

"Mancuso, Mulia, Victor."

Then the *B*'s and *C*'s. "Di Pippo, Garrison, Henry, Palermo, Perez, Sessa, Wilcox."

By the time Malachy gets to the troublemakers and slackers—"Bacotti, Bashinelli, Benevento, Paulino, Prosciutto, Romano, Viscardi"—I know something is very wrong.

She hands Ernie Palmieri his paper with a nod. Tall, green-eyed, and industrious, Ernie's family immigrated from Italy. He has a job working in a *salumeria*; I'm rooting through trash collecting Coke and Pepsi bottles for the five-cent deposits. Ernie, who sits next to me, looks over, pinches his thumb and forefinger, nods his head, and waggles his hand. The message comes across loud and clear: *What's so hard, Coppola? You were born here.*

It hits me: Best for last! Malachy is saving my "Battered War Helmet" for the finale. The pièce de résistance, had I known French.

"Coppola, up here."

"Yes, Sister!"

I bolt out of my seat, Sgt. Stryker charging up Mount Suribachi, Malachy's slights, insults, and cruelty forgotten.

She's standing alongside her oak desk, holding my story, the fluorescent light glinting off her rimless glasses, rendering her pale eyes blank. Grinning, I hold out my hand, half turn to face the class. I never see it coming, a sweeping right-hand punch that knocks me against the blackboard. Then, the billowing sleeves of her brown habit flying, she pounces with a flurry of slaps I'm too stunned to parry. To my shame, tears spring from my eyes in front of the class. In front of Jean.

"Sister?"

"This," she roars, "*is what happens to plagiarists!*"

I don't even know the word.

I was thirteen when I wrote that first story. I never write another until I'm twenty-eight.

That year, Malachy encourages Salvatore Mulia, Dominick D'Alessio, Rosalie DiLorenzo, and a handful of others to apply to Catholic high schools, institutions that by some marvelous alchemy can lift wayward, working-class students onto the path to success. Malachy predicts I'll make "headlines," not the scholarly, scientific, philanthropic, or humanitarian recognition that teachers want for their charges but screaming three-inch Richard Speck tabloid notoriety.

So I study, trekking up to the public library on Sixth Avenue in Park Slope, where I sit surrounded by goofballs in black-framed glasses and homosexuals, all cocked eyebrows and lascivious nods. I don't know *what* to read, so I read everything, all the paperbacks on the rack at the newsstand at Fourth Avenue and Union, convinced science fiction, bodice-rippers, and tales of murderous mau mau are literature. I read milk containers, matchbook covers, comics, whatever floats in front of me.

One earns admission to Catholic high schools by taking the Cooperative Test, a kind of eighth-grade SAT measuring language, reasoning, and math skills. You mark five school choices on the application, and depending on your score you're accepted, rejected, or dumped onto a waiting list. Making three schools is notable; four, outstanding. I don't know anyone who's made five.

Failing has consequences. Manual Training, the neighborhood high school, hands out general diplomas to future ditchdiggers and garbage men. Not a name to inspire confidence. Later rechristened John Jay High School, Manual is the fast track to Rikers Island, and I'm already a legacy student and a troublemaker. My cousin JuJu is remembered for trying to push a piano out the window of Manual's music room; his brothers, Popeye

Anthony and Richie Mel, are outrageous miscreants. This is a competition I want to avoid.

Catholic schools are transformative: St. Francis Prep remakes strapping Irish boys whose immigrant fathers work as groundhogs on the subway system into Notre Dame linemen; Power Memorial transforms Ferdinand Lewis Alcindor into NBA superstar Kareem Abdul-Jabbar, a bitter experience that stays with him for the rest of his life. Bishop Loughlin incubates Rudy Giuliani, whose father is serving time in Sing Sing, into "America's mayor" and then something else. La Salle, the Jesuit military academy in Midtown, Manhattan, educates Antonin Scalia and the Seventh Avenue subway "Commandos." St. Augustine, tuition underwritten by local parishes, produces Governor Hugh Carey.

I take the Cooperative Test on a Saturday, needle-sharp No. 2 pencils at the ready. I'm careful to keep my answers to the multiple-choice questions within the little circles. The waiting begins all over again. Over the next six weeks, I race home for lunch, where Gloria invariably serves pork and beans and fried eggs.

"Ma, the mailman come?"

"Yes."

"Any mail?"

"No."

"You sure?"

"Jesus!"

"Ma, it's important."

Our mailman, a Black man nicknamed "Brownie," dwells within Gowanus's magic circle. No one, not the most reckless junkie, dares trouble him. Of course, Brownie is perfectly tailored to our needs. He manages *not* to deliver overdue rent bills, car payment notes, subpoenas, and IRS notices—marking them "return to sender." At Christmas, everyone takes care of him.

One morning, word spreads that the test results are in. I race home, dodging Butchie, the lisping patrol boy who works the corner of Third Avenue and Carroll Street, darting between trucks and tractor trailers. I duck down the three concrete steps to our basement apartment, shoulder the hollow plywood front door like Sam Huff, sending the red ribbon of sleigh bells we use as a doorbell jangling.

Gloria is standing there, a sheaf of envelopes in her hand. There are five—St. Augustine, Brooklyn Prep, Xaverian, St. Leonard, and St. Francis Prep—typed and sealed in starch-white envelopes. She hands them to me, then steps away, allowing me the moment.

An atheist, I mumble a prayer and tear them open.

Five schools. I've made five schools!

I stumble outside onto the sidewalk. In Gowanus, life is lived on the street. Gloria follows, puts her arms around me.

"I'm so proud!" She's thirty-eight years old and loves her sons beyond measure. "I'll call your father. He'll be so happy."

Tommy and Joey are clinging to my legs. We spin round and round on the sidewalk.

Fat Rosie lumbers across Carroll Street, her flowered muumuu billowing like a dhow. Rosie spends mornings sitting under a metal awning—her name emblazoned on it—gossiping, afternoons taking "the numbers" from Puerto Rican factory workers in Industry City. Emo, her boyfriend, a man with a gambling problem, was recently found suspended from a meat hook in Bensonhurst. Rosie keeps his collection of stuffed animals. She kisses me, smearing white lipstick on my cheek, then takes my hand, stuffing a ten-dollar bill into my palm.

"Glad somebody in this fucking neighborhood ain't a moron!"

Across the street, Ernie is standing next to Uncle Honey in front of Monte's restaurant.

"How'd ya do?" I shout.

"Made St. Leonard."

"Watch them fag priests!" says Honey as I walk up. "*Mammone*, how 'bout you?"

"I made five."

"Whoa!"

Honey reaches into his pocket, peels two twenties off a roll of bills, hands them to us.

"Congratulations. Yous two will get an education. Yous won't have to break your ass every day like me."

Ernie pumps his closed fist, mock masturbation. Honey laughs, amused at his own bullshit. He pretend slaps both of us.

"Get the fuck out of here!"

A line of students wavers outside the convent on Whitwell Place. Malachy is eating lunch on the convent's brick porch, congratulating the eighth graders as they come by. I join the line. Sal is already on the porch, behind him, Kathleen Victor and Dominick D'Alessio.

"I bet you did good." Jean appears alongside me, an apparition. She's as tall as I am, with blue eyes and wavy chestnut hair. The top two buttons of her uniform blouse are undone.

"He made all five schools!" Ernie blurts.

"Wow!" says Jean. "That's great!"

I blush.

"Give him a kiss!" Ernie chortles.

And she does. In front of the line of students, she puts her hand gently around my neck and pulls me close.

"You're not like the rest of us," she whispers.

I've never kissed, never touched a girl, have never known the perfume of an adolescent female. I stand there, experiencing and trying to remember at the same time. The freckled Henry twins, Carolyn and Carol Ann, wolf-whistle. Malachy looks up and frowns. I step onto the porch where Sal, Rosalie DiLorenzo, and Dominick D'Alessio stand alongside the bulky nun like courtiers.

She's eating baked fish, boiled potatoes, and slices of a purple-red vegetable I haven't seen before.

"Ernest, for your poor mother's sake," Malachy says, "I hope some Christian school was willing to take on the burden of your education."

"St. Leonard!" says Ernie.

"Will wonders never cease?"

It will be a short-lived miracle. Ernie is thrown out of St. Leonard's a year later for vandalizing a subway car. A pompadoured 250-pound fifteen-year-old wearing the distinctive green-and-yellow St. Leonard jacket is hard to forget.

Malachy turns to me. I catch a whiff of her, pissy and sour beneath the starched brown habit, her breath rank with onions and fish.

"Kathleen Victor, Mr. Mulia, and Rosalie DiLorenzo were accepted by four high schools. Aren't you proud of them? Do you see the rewards hard work can bring?"

Sal grins, clasping his hands above his head like a fighter.

"I made five," I say. "St. Augustine too. I'm gonna go there."

Startled, Sal hesitates, then walks up, puts his right hand behind my neck, and shoves me affectionately.

"All right!" he says.

"Good job, Vinny." This from Kathleen Victor, smart as a whip and no Malachy favorite.

I have a little speech prepared, thanking Malachy for being my teacher, saying that she's "tough but fair." I open my mouth. The nun puts down her fork, shoots a glance at Jean and the Henry twins standing at the edge of the porch.

"You don't deserve it, Coppola," she says. "I know you for the sneak and the cheat that you are."

I flinch. This is worse than any beating.

"Sister!" Kathleen gasps.

I stand there, eyes fixed on the table, feeling heat rising in my chest. A fly makes its way across the checkered tablecloth.

"Excuse me . . ."

I turn. Jean is standing at the top porch step. I brush past her, trip, catch myself, and begin running, daring my ravaged heart to explode. Block after block I run, past the old powerhouse, the lot filled with leaking barrels of toxic chemicals, slowing only when I cross the Third Street Bridge over the Gowanus Canal.

By then, I'm in another neighborhood.

CHAPTER TWO

Shoot the Undertaker

On a summer morning, eight-year-old Anthony Stuto skips through the gate of his family's house at 441 Carroll Street, turns right, and heads straight for the canal where his friends wait. Playing on the bank, Anthony trips on a stringpiece, one of the rotting rectangular timbers lining the waterway, and plunges ten feet into the foul water. He'd been warned—as we all would be—to stay away. No one ever listens, drawn by the siren song of clanking drawbridges, the nasal honk of tugboats' air horns, the rippling strings of barges carrying fuel oil and coal, all just yards from our houses.

Anthony drowns.

This is 1915. Gowanus is the frontier. Thousands of southern Italians are flooding in, displacing fleeing Irish and Germans, eager to get a feel for what's possible in this "America." My great-grandfather Salvatore Giordano and his seven sons are among them. Oddly, the *uomini di rispetto* are neither mafiosi nor politicians, but undertakers, seemingly a respectable, reliable, and sedate profession. But competition is fierce, furious, cutthroat. "People are dying," as the joke has it, "to get into the cemetery," but not many, or fast enough.

Anthony Stuto's corpse triggers a riot. From Union Street, undertaker Gaetano Mangano, who's building a powerful political machine in the Eighth Ward, lands the funeral, but when he arrives to collect the boy's body, rowdy, rough-hewn John Romanelli is lying in wait. Imprecations are exchanged, knives pulled, shots fired. Mangano is shot *and* stabbed, seemingly mortally wounded. One of Gaetano's minions fires a pistol point-blank at Romanelli but misses. Undaunted, Romanelli chases his assailant to Union Street, where a policeman named Siegel puts a bullet through the shooter's hat.

All hell breaks loose. On August 8, the *Times Union*, an Albany, New York, paper, reports, "A riot call was sent to the Bergen Street station and all the reserves turned out. About 30,000 [*sic*] Italians were found swarming the streets wildly excited and the police had their hands full restoring order. No one seemed to know who shot Mangano."

Mangano survives and thrives. His son, Assemblyman James V. Mangano, is the political boss who dispenses patronage, handpicks officeholders, and solves "neighborhood needs" through the 1970s. He will resolve the conflict between local Italians and the Hare Krishna cult who arrive on Henry Street in the 1960s. Gaetano's grandson Guy Mangano is elected to the New York Supreme Court in 1979.

✦ ✦ ✦

In 1919, John Romanelli, the self-proclaimed "mayor of the Italian community," sells ten drums of embalming fluid to bootleggers in the Bronx who cut, color, ship, and sell it as moonshine in Hartford and New Haven, Connecticut, and Chicopee Falls, Massachusetts. More than one hundred men and women die or are blinded. Romanelli serves two years in Sing Sing and returns to Gowanus.

In the sixties, I hang out in an upstairs apartment in Romanelli's funeral parlor on President Street with his great-grandson. We lure girls into the basement embalming room, then turn out the lights and lock the doors leaving them shrieking among sheeted, toe-tagged corpses.

CHAPTER THREE

Fly-Fishing on the Gowanus

"In nomine Patris et Filio et Spiritu Sancti."

"A-men."

Sister Mary Malachy crosses herself as she intones the prayer, thrusting her prognathous jaw forward, an inquisitor ready to swoop down on the budding apostates in her charge. She tugs at the sleeve of her brown habit, taps the Timex watch on her thick wrist. Across her desk, thirty-five eighth graders shift to attention, ink-stained fingers reaching for rosaries.

She studies us—ice-blue eyes behind rimless glasses half-closed in feigned prayer—alert to every exhalation of breath, every shoe scuff, sigh, and stomach rumble. Malachy knows that behind our frayed white shirts and clip-on ties, beneath the pleated skirts and Peter Pan collars, we dream only of stickball and lipstick, of stink bombs, dirty pictures, fireworks, rotten eggs, Frankie Avalon, Ringolevio, and kick the can. She knows the boys—the Italians—will touch the giggling girls in the darkness of the cloakroom, make them squeal in the crowded stairwells as they march from the schoolyard after lunch.

Malachy wears a wedding band signifying her marriage to Jesus Christ and her renunciation of pleasure. Pain is another matter. She will spare no effort driving us up the slippery slopes of Salvation. This is her purpose, the vocation that carried her from the bottle-green glens of Donegal to this vale of tears, this Golgotha.

She nods to a dark-skinned girl in a raveled green sweater in the fourth row, her mouth ripe and red as original sin.

"The First Sorrowful Mystery, the Agony in the Garden," Rosa Perez begins.

"Our Father, who art in heaven, hallowed be thy name . . ."

The class murmurs the response, voices echoing down tiled corridors, merging with the morning prayers of other students like the drone of honeybees. The rosary continues, the *hallowed be*s and *Holy Ghost*s as dry as the husks of dead insects. In the fifth row, Jean W inhales—her ripening breasts strain against her blouse—and announces the Second Sorrowful Mystery.

An aisle away, I hunch over my catechism penciling a dove, the representation of the Holy Ghost, shitting on the head of Pope Pius XII. A feral creature, I sense a predator's approach. I count heads.

"Ten . . . Eleven . . . Twelve . . . Shit!"

It's my turn to proclaim the next mystery.

"The Third Sorrowful Mystery?" I mouth the question, prompting my brain to supply an answer. Nothing.

Ascensions. Assumptions. Redemptions.

Heaven sounds like a cheap furniture store.

Mysteries swim in my head. Malachy will have me

scrubbing the church basement, the labyrinth where Brother Masseo lurks among the broken statues of martyrs and serpents. Three more *Hail Mary*s ratchet by. I crank my head left, cough, then whisper, "What's the Third Mystery?"

"Ya mother's box," Sal replies.

"Don't fool around!"

"Her canary."

Ernie snorts, the sound among the murmurs loud as a breaching whale. Malachy's wimpled head rotates. I duck, disappearing like, I imagine, Jonah into the belly of the Leviathan.

"Come on. Please!"

The nun fills the aisle between the rows of bolted-down desks. She advances, seeming to sniff the air. Sal hunches over his beads, a monk lost in divine rapture.

"Hail Mary, full of grace . . ." A drone four seats in front of me.

I squeeze my Italian rosary, a gift from Vincenzo, my grandfather. A tiny window in the crucifix reveals a bone chip floating in holy water like a carpenter's level. I clench the holy bone.

"Please, Jesus . . . I'll . . ." I hesitate. "I won't . . ."

A vision of Jean blossoms in my head, plaid uniform skirt inching up, revealing her coltish thighs. I sigh, steady myself for the charge. Instinctively, my hand rises to the fading purple bruise under my left eye.

In the corner by the whistling radiators, Tommy Cacasotte stirs. The bolts holding his desk to the polished oak floor squeal in protest. Malachy sneers at him. Stained tie, frayed white shirt, gray work pants straining against his ass like sausage casing, he's a mockery of all that is pure, clean, Christlike. Father Mario and the Franciscans of Our Lady of Peace Parish count the days until New York State law allows them to discharge "Shit the Pants" like so much sewage into the gutter.

Tommy's internal clock is chiming noon. Soon he'll eat a hero sandwich at his mother Margherita's (pronounced, in our dialect, "Ma-ga-la's") Third Avenue grocery, waddle home, root into his unmade bed. At five thirty p.m., the *Mickey Mouse Club* theme will stir him to masturbation.

Tommy lifts his ass and farts, a lament from his bowels that derails the Holy Rosary and wreathes the classroom in silence. The fallout stops Malachy as she's about to pull me from my seat. Rows of students surge forward, surfers riding a wave, coughing, pretend-gagging, holding their throats. Shrieking, they sweep past me, past Malachy, out the front door.

The lunch bell clangs. I stand, lock eyes with her.

"The Third Sorrowful Mystery!" I shout, slapping Sal's still bowed head. "The Crowning with Thorns!"

I swivel right, dash forward and out the door. I fly down the metal steps, out of the building, dodge Butchie the Fag, the patrol boy, and the thundering trucks on Third Avenue, race down Carroll Street past my house, past Jimmy the Morgue's idling Buick Electra, past Monte's, and the John P. Carlson ink factory. I stand at the canal's gray railing, the pale sun caressing my face.

In Monte's, Sonny the Indian sips brown whiskey and watches me race down the sidewalk, feinting garbage cans, my gangly body struggling to keep up with my brain. He stares at the long mirror above the bar, lifts his chin. Whose face is it? What purpose the bunched muscles and tendons of the formidable jaw? The questions chase themselves behind his impassive eyes.

After a moment, he grunts, "More whiskey."

Fifteen minutes later, I walk back up Carroll Street.

A month earlier, at the Grand Army Plaza Library, a woman with a face like parchment had shown me sketches depicting the Gowanus estuary in the 1600s. Apple trees flourished along its banks. The Gowanus oyster was renowned for its size and abundance; they were exported to Amsterdam and London.

I describe these wonders to Ernie and Sal.

"Go fuck yourself!"

Engulfed in a cloud of sautéing garlic and simmering tomatoes emanating from Monte's Venetian Room, I float above the cobblestone street, imagining verdant hills rolling past what is now Carroll Gardens and Cobble Hill, to the Heights above New York Harbor. Seventeenth-century ships at anchor bob in the sunlight at the foot of Wall Street.

Crack!

A slap off the back of my head ends my meditation. Honey and Ernie, his nephew, are standing in front of Monte's. Holding a thick Cuban cigar, Honey is grinning. Sonny is to his left, Easter Island in a leather trench coat. Shaky stands to his right and glares malevolently at me.

"Daydreaming, you mope?" says Honey.

"What?" I mumble.

"You hungry? Go inside. Red'll make you a sammich."

"No. I'm fasting."

"It ain't Lent. Think them cocksucker priests fast? Bullshit!"

"Fasting makes you think better. In India . . ."

"Sonny's an Indian. He don't fast."

Sonny studies his whiskey and says nothing.

"What happened to your face?" says Honey. "Your father go to work on you again?"

Uncomfortable, I look at Ernie. "You ready?"

"Yous better smarten up," Honey warns. "Yous ain't kids no more."

He waves his cigar, digs into his pocket, and pulls out a thick roll. He peels off two five-dollar bills.

"Get some ice creams. You, Vinny, bring me the *News* and the *Mirror.* Don't forget like last time."

"I won't. I promise." (*I'm rich!*)

"That Irish twat still giving yous trouble?"

"She hates us."

"She hates Vinny 'cause he's smart," says Ernie.

"I ain't smart!"

I tilt my head toward the bridge. We begin inching away.

"Where yous a-goin'?" Honey jerks his thumb toward Third Ave. "School's that way."

"We don't gotta be back till one o'clock."

"Stay away from that fucking canal!" Honey spreads his stubby arms. "They got water rats this big! All kind of shit. Yous a-gonna get rabies. Something happens, I'll give yous the rest! Stay outta dere!"

Shaky walks out of the restaurant, greasy pompadour and pockmarked face.

"Yo, Honey, you got a call. Carmine."

Honey groans.

He and Sonny walk into Monte's, leaving Shaky standing there.

Ernie stage-whispers, "Looks like a dog shit on his head."

I giggle.

Shaky turns, shoots me a look. "Whatta yous looking at?"

"Nothing. I . . ."

"Jerkoffs, I'll go to work on both of yous! You, you fat slob, don't think your uncle can stop me neither."

"We're talking about school," says Ernie. "Ever hear of it?"

Shaky pulls a wad of bills out of his pants pocket. "School is for jerkoffs."

Ernie grabs his balls. "Fuhgeddaboudit!"

We dart between a row of parked cars, then head for the Carroll Street Bridge, a rare and decaying architectural jewel. Twenty yards from the water, it hits us, the wretched blend of raw sewage, chemical spills, oil from sunken barges and abandoned cars, garbage, feces, grease, bloated carcasses of dogs floating in and out on the tide. In the 1960s, you can drive a car at fifty miles per hour down Carroll Street from Hoyt, accelerate over the one-hundred-foot-wide waterway—and gag.

We cut left alongside the ink factory. On the bank, Sal and Rocco are already stripping thin, whiplike branches from the ailanthus trees that somehow thrive along the canal. Short and dark-complected, Rocco is dressed like the accountant he'll never be, tweed overcoat, wool pants, polished shoes, white shirt stiff with starch, blue tie held in place by a fake pearl.

I pull my rod from my hiding place in the weeds, a McCrory five-and-dime reproduction of the ones I see in *Field & Stream.* I sense a larger world that I want to be part of, so I cultivate mail-order hobbies: stamp and coin collections, a rock collection—shards of industrial glass and brick fragments I mistake for quartz and feldspar, bright chemical crystals scavenged from the Golten Marine Company's abandoned facility near the canal. Red plastic rockets powered by compressed air and water designed for kids in cornfields. A month until they arrive in the mail, then one launch and they disappear over the rooftops.

I tie on a sinker and outsize hook.

"High tide. Fishing's gonna be good."

Sal finishes stripping his branch and runs to the ten-foot diameter stone culvert that carries waste from our toilets and sewers directly into the water.

He reaches down and begins trolling. Rocco picks a spot alongside a half-sunken barge smeared with oil and grease. Ernie elbows in front of him.

"Thanks for helping me . . . you jerk!"

"Swear to God," Sal mumbles. "I don't know the stupid mystery!"

"'Swear to God,'" I mimic. "Some friend!"

"Screw you!"

"Got one!" This from Rocco.

"That's mines!" says Ernie. "Slippery bastids!"

Rocco hauls an eight-inch condom from the water.

"All right!" Sal says. "Whitefish!"

Putrescent water splashes Rocco's pants as he manipulates the dripping tube onto a tire. Nearby, seven fly-buzzed condoms, Tuesday's catch, shrivel in the sun.

"I got two!" shouts Ernie lifting his branch from the water.

"Your mama was busy!" Sal shouts.

I watch a dead cat float by in the water. For the next ten minutes, I concentrate, keen as Hemingway in a trout stream in the Pyrenees. Finally, I spot a rubber discharged ("released") from the culvert. I carefully pluck it out of the water. Sal is bent over examining the catch of the day. I circle. Ernie sees me, backs away. I put a finger to my lips, creep closer, closer, and lay the dripping thing on Sal's shoulder.

"Somebody I want you to meet . . ."

He looks up. "Wha . . . ?"

I throw down my fishing rod, dart away.

"Eccch! *Schifoso!*" Ernie shouts, pointing.

"What?"

Sal whirls once, twice, a dog chasing its tail. The condom leaves a snail track on his coat. By then, I'm thirty feet away, giggling, running among the piles of slag and bricks, heading for a path that winds through a salvage yard and back out onto Carroll Street.

Sal, a runner, throws his raincoat at Rocco. "My mother will kill me! I'll kill you!"

I climb a towering mound of garbage, turn, and give him the finger. "The First Sorrowful Mystery," I scream. "Your fucked-up coat!"

I lose my footing, skitter down the other side. Scramble to my feet, duck behind another pile of trash, accelerate toward a hole in the fence one hundred feet away. I trip over a roll of discarded linoleum, almost regain my balance—there's broken glass, rebar, cinder blocks scattered like a minefield—then fall hard in front of a mountain of blue metal drums piled along the fence.

"Ahh!"

Instinctively, I burrow between two barrels.

In the distance, the bells of Our Lady of Peace Parish chime the Angelus, then ring the hour, a single note that reverberates in my metal womb like a funeral knell. One o'clock! I crawl deeper, already imagining a pirate cave formed by the rusting drums, instantly forgetting about school and rats and packs of feral dogs. I find myself in a small clearing surrounded by drums leaching yellow powder. I stand up, notice my grease-stained school pants. Ruined.

"Shit!"

A brown paper bag rests against one of the drums. I walk closer, reach down, and pick it up, disappointed at how light it feels. Neighborhood junkies who burglarize Cambie's Trucking and other Gowanus companies hide their swag in the lots that are our fiefdoms. We steal from thieves, expropriating expensive handbags, perfume, and shoes for our mothers. Once, we find a Carrier air-conditioning unit still in its packing crate.

A pillowcase is stuffed inside the bag. I pull it out. Stained a dark, clotty red.

"Jesus!" I fling the bag away with both hands.

The October wind, heavy with salt from the harbor, cuts through my thin jacket. I sniffle, wipe my nose on my sleeve. Acrid smoke—truck tires constantly burning in Smoky Joe's junkyard next door—fouls the air. I look up, see the sun reflected in the back windows of tenements. I remind myself I'm just fifty yards from my own backyard. Gloria is in the kitchen doing lunch dishes, trying to figure out what to cook for supper on her meager budget.

I walk over to the pillowcase and kick. The bloody cloth unravels.

Something flies out.

"Whaa!" I gasp.

I step closer. A tiny clawlike hand. Closer. A baby, smaller than one of Goldie's plucked chickens, blackened, smeared with blood and dirt. A naked dark-haired boy, one arm reaching up to the empty sky.

"Ahhh!"

I turn and duck back through the tunnel of barrels,

bile rising in my throat. I'm trying not to gag when Sal leaps onto my back. I fall to the ground gasping, spinning wildly, legs pinwheeling. In a second, he's kneeling on my chest, forcing my arms back.

"Stop!"

He's holding a dried condom to rub in my face.

"Please stop!"

"Fucking baby cry," Sal says, relenting. "You ruined my coat."

We crawl together into the clearing and stand over the thing. I want to pick the child up and cradle it in my arms. Or I tell myself I want to. Sal looks at me like I'm crazy. The tiny body shudders, but I'm the one trembling.

"It was alive."

Sal tries to cover it with the pillowcase. Fails.

"We don't say nothing to nobody. Right?"

"I don't know. This is . . . this is a sin."

A rock clangs against the steel drums. We both scream. A second stone lands at my feet. A moment later, Ernie squeezes into the clearing.

"Ya two *mammoni*! What'd yous steal?"

He's laughing, rubbing his right thumb across the tip of his forefinger, the Neapolitan sign for a thief. And then he sees.

"Aggh! The fuck is that?"

He backs away, holding his hands in front of his face.

"We found it."

"*Schifosos!* It's got germs. You'll get sick."

A stream of vomit, bits of Monte's pasta and pastry clearly visible, shoots out of Ernie's mouth.

Ten minutes later, we walk out of the lot, chilled, smeared with grime, two hours late for school. Sister Mary Malachy waiting to spell *O-B-E-D-I-E-N-C-E* on my knuckles with a round oak pointer that whistles as it cuts through the air.

Halfway up the block Ernie says, “You know it belongs to somebody?”

“Whaddya mean?”

“Somebody got rid of it . . . on purpose.”

“Threw a baby away?”

He looks at us like we’re idiots. “It ain’t a baby.”

“Bullshit!”

“It’s a . . . a fetal. My sister Lucille has these pictures . . .”

“Of what?”

“A fetal. A baby that ain’t been born . . . Taken out of a girl’s stomach.”

“Get out of here!”

“What for?”

“Because the girl ain’t married or don’t want it or . . .”

“That’s murder!”

Ernie shoots me a furious look. “Don’t say that! It’s like a business . . . Yous could get us a lot of trouble. I ain’t kidding.”

“Fuck the cops!”

“I ain’t talking about cops!”

“What trouble?” I ask, glancing at Sal. “Over some little nigger baby?”

“It ain’t a nigger!” Ernie shouts. “Yous know it ain’t a nigger!”

We did know, and I’d like to say it didn’t matter. Limbo—the place where souls remain that cannot enter heaven—is located on the border of hell, a working definition of Gowanus. Baptism matters. Extreme Unction matters. Truth matters, I tell myself over and over again in the next weeks.

CHAPTER FOUR

The Lonesome Death of Louie the Fag

The light blinks green at Sixth Street and Third Avenue. The car explodes, tires squealing, racing parallel to the Gowanus, flying over the bridge and past the light at Third Street, already accelerating past sixty miles per hour. Maybe a Chevelle SS or GTO—make and model blurred by velocity and the deafening roar echoing off factory walls.

The driver, most likely escaped from the grimy Puerto Rican tenements on the far side of Hamilton Avenue, and doubtless animated—as I am—by poverty and rage and otherness, is racing toward the Williamsburgh Bank, the phallic thirty-seven-story tombstone looming over South Brooklyn.

The driver seems oblivious to the teeming sidewalks and streets shimmering in the heat, the little girls skipping rope on the cracked sidewalks; he's certainly unaware of Louie the Fag, who's climbed wearily up the steps of the Union Street subway station.

✦ ✦ ✦

In the 1960s, Gowanus was still a community plucked from the desolate triangle of crumbling villages and towns outside of Naples and deposited like weeds along the canal's pestilent banks: Nocera, Tramonti, Scafati, Pagani, and Eboli, a place so forlorn, legend has it that it stopped Christ the Redeemer in his tracks. Castellammare di Stabia was Al Capone's ancestral home, but Capone, despite his Chicago pedigree, was born at 38 Garfield Place, two blocks from my house. I can't say why, but I'm very proud of this fact. The bullet holes in the doorway of a long-shuttered bar on Fourth Avenue are practically a religious shrine marking the spot where Frank "Frankie Shots" Abbatemarco was . . . shot.

My grandparents immigrated from Pagani, 140 miles and light-years from Rome. Al Pagano ran the local hardware store where nails were stored in wooden barrels and sold by the pennyweight. Thirty-five first cousins live within three blocks of my house. My mother's family, the Giordanos, serve Sunday afternoon dinner—spaghetti, braciole; bubbling pots of minestra, pork ribs, salt pork, prosciutto, escarole, broccoli rabe; delicate seafood salads, shrimp, calamari, baby octopus, clams; *stoccu*, rehydrated codfish baked with olives, capers, and tomatoes, so intense the smell drives me from my grandmother's kitchen—on a long table on the sidewalk at the corner of Nevins and Carroll. I can practically ask the driver of an idling car to pass the meatballs. Grown-ups drink homemade wine sweetened with peaches Old Man Stuto sells for three dollars a gallon.

After half a century in Brooklyn, the old families—Russo,

Persico, Giordano, Lauro, Stuto, Barbella, Christiano, Manzo—are so intertwined and intermarried as to be indistinguishable, a community bound by blood, ethnicity, organized crime, and distrust of anyone—priest, police, politician—beyond the canal banks, a magic circle, often irrational and violent but tender and intensely protective of its own.

Three formerly institutionalized psychotics, and two horribly inbred brothers—creatures from the canal's black lagoon—wander the streets with the suffix *-pazzo* ("crazy") pinned to their names like donkey tails. "Dent in the head" is another suffix; it's hilarious in dialect Italian.

Maggie, a World War II widow, thinks she hears the tap-tap-tapping of "niggers on the roof." Sonny the Indian, a Native American who fled a community of Mohawk ironworkers living in Boerum Hill, wants to be in the Mafia. No one thinks of institutionalizing these folk. We're ahead of the societal curve.

Louie the Fag is ten years older than me. He wears his salt-and-pepper hair short, Caesar-style. I sport a curly pompadour. I wear a leather coat; he, a black cotton jacket. Louie works a dead-end job in a department store on Fulton Street. I'm hoping to go to college. He's gay, though the term doesn't yet exist. Not *swishy*, not a *fairy*, words used in those days. Two drag queens, Sarah and Sally, predatory hairdressers from Fifth Avenue, fill that bill. Butchie the Fag (no relation to Louie), captain of the patrol boys at Our Lady of Peace Elementary School, has a flaming scarlet streak in his hair, a leading indicator of sexual orientation. When I tease him, Butchie beats the shit out of me in front of the Capri Club in full view of half a dozen laughing wiseguys. Unknown to me, my kid brother, Thomas, is gay. Twenty years later, his AIDS diagnosis will destroy our family.

Louie is teased, but not beaten or tormented. It's simply how things are. My cousin Joseph Tramontano, one of the few men in the neighborhood with a college degree, is dubbed "Professor Beans" (i.e., education amounts to a "hill of beans"). Three-hundred-pound Jimmy the Morgue works nights at Kings County Hospital, so he's rumored to be a necrophiliac. I never explore that sobriquet further. Hugh "Mac" McIntosh kills people. I'm a reader, not a valuable skill set, so I'm labeled "Vinny the Boob."

Louie eats hero sandwiches with us in Otto's Social Club, plays pinochle, brisk (briscola), and gin rummy, drives with us to Coney Island on warm summer nights for Nathan's hot dogs. I never catch a sexual vibe from him, though I'm certainly not privy to the inner man. He lives with his mother, has nieces and nephews, is my cousin Jerry "Alibi Ike"'s best friend. Louie is from the neighborhood. That, more than sexual orientation, defines him. Louie was liberated long before the 1969 Stonewall riots and dwells, however uncomfortably, inside the magic circle.

✦ ✦ ✦

The machine, thundering past First Street, is now something monstrous, a reanimated thing, engine snarling, exhaust thundering, front end leaping as the driver, hunched over the steering wheel, shifts into fourth gear. Buffalo Manzo, grilling Italian sausages on a steel drum, looks up as the wave of sound engulfs him. Dean Martin, blasting from the jukebox outside the Capri Club, is drowned out. Gamblers gathered around a parked car's radio strain to hear Cappy Caposella call the Aqueduct results. On Carroll Street, the stoplight in front of Tony's Barberhop gleams green.

Louie has reached Romanelli's Funeral Home at the corner of President and Third Avenue. He glances up at the newly installed stoplight. I'm halfway down President Street outside Otto's Social Club, joking with Peter L. My three younger brothers are scattered in the schoolyards and empty lots that are our playgrounds. Gloria has finished her Saturday-morning shopping at Spinner's supermarket on "the Avenue," Fifth Avenue. The stretch between Flatbush and Third Street is dotted with abandoned shops and dying mom-and-pop businesses. Fifty years later, the street will come back again bustling with hipsters, wine bars, and upscale trattorias.

My father, a longshoreman like most neighborhood men, is working overtime at the Black Diamond Lines' pier in Red Hook. Women, young and old, are sitting outside their houses on vinyl and chrome kitchen chairs, some rocking baby carriages, others knitting the sequined hats commissioned by an enterprising wholesaler named Jennie Pentangelo from Nevins Street. Teenage girls—corpse-white lipstick is in style, and it drives me wild—are sitting in halters and tight shorts on the stoops, listening to AM radio and discussing boys other than me. Young kids, some with the faces of Botticelli angels, dart between parked cars, teasing and punching and hurling idiotic insults.

Unlike the sepulchral streets above Sixth Avenue, noise is constant on Third Avenue: bellowing tractor trailers making their way to Atlantic Avenue from the piers; the B37 bus, brakes squealing, fatalistic kids hitching on its back bumpers, exhaust fumes blowing in their faces; the

Four Seasons shrieking "Rag Doll" from Johnny DiMucci's yellow Electra 225 convertible; Black gangbangers with do-rags and lye straighteners plastering their heads, blasting soul music from eggplant-colored Caddies; the singsong Italian of Jumbo Angioletti the fruit peddler; Con Edison trucks hauling groaning spools of cable (one chops my cousin JuJu's fingers right off when he hitches a ride).

The driver is doing one hundred miles per hour when he passes the Glory Social Club, roughly 150 feet per second. When the light on President Street turns red, he doesn't see it, can't react, or jams the gas pedal to the floor and runs right fucking through it. At that instant, Louie has one second to live. I imagine him stepping off the curb, maybe spotting his mother walking up President Street, the hint of a smile forming on his lips. Parked cars blind him to approaching death.

Perhaps he's thinking of nothing at all.

Half a block away, I hear thunder echoing off the cars lined bumper to bumper along Third Avenue—a roar, a snarl, and then a sickening sound like no other. Years later, when an old man in pajamas jumps out the twentieth-floor window of a Brooklyn Heights hotel and lands ten feet in front of me, I hear someone describe that sound as "a watermelon thrown off a tall ladder." I whirl—we all do—and see a figure soaring over the arm of the light pole as cleanly as a kicked field goal. But for the sound, it could have been a straw man, old jeans and a stuffed shirt made during the World Series and hung from lampposts to deride the Yankees.

The car never even slows. It blows past Union Street and is gone. When I reach the corner, twenty people are gathered in a wobbly circle, and more are coming.

The body is slumped face down. A viscous corona forms around the skull; black chinos are half pulled down from the impact, the obscenity of death. A minute goes by, seems like an hour; no one dares approach the lonesome, lifeless thing on the asphalt. No one dares claim it for their own. Then women begin shrieking out names.

"Richie?"

"Funzi?"

"Sally?"

I step closer. Closer still. My friend Peter, who'll die way too young, seizes my arm in his iron grip. His face is all wrong. He thinks it's my father.

"Come on," he says. "Let's get the fuck out of here."

"Peter . . ."

I can't finish. Thick salt-and-pepper hair, black cotton jacket, the scuffed work shoes, the blood. I pull away, run the short block to Carroll Street, turn right, heart pounding, dodging cars. I burst through our unlocked door, the ribbon of bells jangling.

"Mom?"

No answer.

"Mom!"

She's gone. I jerk open the closet door and begin tearing through coats and jackets and blouses. My father's black jacket is missing. Shouting, I run in and out of neighbors' houses, up and down creaking staircases. No answer, no Gloria, no one home.

Sobbing, I walk slowly back to President Street. I must keep my brothers away. A siren wails in the distance. I burst through the magic circle, now a bulwark against the outside world. It's deathly quiet.

Louie's mother is kneeling by his side.

Attempting to shield him, she turns his head.

CHAPTER FIVE

The Beast in the Basement

I feel his presence. Ten years old, I'm standing at the urinal in the deserted second-floor boys' lavatory. The ammonia smell is overpowering. I unzip my pants, flip my brown clip-on tie over my shoulder. I look up; he's watching, a balding middle-aged man dressed in the brown robes of a Franciscan. "Where did he come from?" I wonder and scuttle back to class. I'm innocent and unaware of the tunnel running from the back of the church altar to my elementary school bathroom. Had I been aware, I'd have imagined secret passages, golden chalices, Galahad, the Holy Grail, saints, dragons, and monsters.

The monster is real: Brother Masseo Butteri, director of the Altar Boys' Society at Our Lady of Peace, my church, my school, my parish. In Masseo, the corruption, perversion, and hypocrisy poisoning the Catholic Church is made flesh. Masseo rapes his charges, my best friend among them, operating boldly, clerical collar rendering him invisible to parents and administrators. At Christmas, his voice booms above all others, singing, "O

Bambino, mio divino." He operates recklessly, just outside the gazes of men like Snake and Slush who would kill him for what he does to children.

It's a simpler time. The Church is powerful, omnipresent, unquestioned. I awaken to the tolling of church bells, comforting and discordant. Parochial schools educate me. Catholic charities take my candy money. I cross the poisonous Gowanus delivering *The Tablet*, a Catholic newspaper that publishes lists of "Legion of Decency" movies I can't see, books I can't read, thoughts I can't think under the pain of hell. On the Feast of Saint Francis, I jostle for the loaves of holy bread Masseo hands out at the altar. I'm repelled by the stench of his rotting teeth. Young mothers, a generation removed from Naples and Palermo, dress olive-skinned preschoolers in Franciscan robes as Masseo watches.

No one questions why Pastor Mario Ciampi drinks with wiseguys in Monte's restaurant. Or why Ciampi's successor Arthur Lattanzi, a priest with a Vince Lombardi complex, converts our recreation center, paid for by impoverished immigrants, into a training camp for his football squads—and locks local kids out. Like them, Masseo operates in a moral vacuum. He targets the youngest, most vulnerable, most innocent. The boys graduate and move on, shame and secrets locked inside, eating at them for decades. But there are whispers.

I dream of being an altar boy. I want to dress in medieval robes, chant dead languages, strike melodious bells, swing censers filled with burning incense in front of Jean W as she kneels at the altar, tongue extended for Communion. Altar boys play poker and briscola, eat pizza and chicken in the basket in the sacristy. Giggling, they bite through three-inch stacks of unconsecrated hosts that taste like Satellite Wafers' penny candy. I live in my head; they go on field trips to Coney Island's Raven Hall and Washington Baths, swim naked in the Hotel Saint George's saltwater pool under a mirrored ceiling, unaware of the grown men leering and pleasuring themselves in the balcony. They spend weekends at a leafy Franciscan retreat upstate in Wappingers Falls, share scary stories about Halloween night in the pitch-dark church basement. Outside, I celebrate Halloween by beating my friends with stockings filled with powdered chalk.

I want to escape the fantasy that is my life. In the seventh grade, I'm named captain of the patrol boys, a commission that ends abruptly when the PTA president decides "captain" would enhance her son's high school applications. Sister Mary Malachy orders me to turn in the blue badge and the white Sam Browne belt I've scrubbed with Ajax in Gloria's kitchen sink.

The PTA president's son is one of the boys molested by Masseo.

Masseo takes his name from St. Francis's most beloved disciple. In Gowanus, Brother Masseo's hand is everywhere, but we're too busy, too poor, too young, too cowed, or too distracted to see. Raven Hall and Washington Baths are popular hangouts for the homosexuals of the era; pedophiles rule the Saint George Hotel pool. In Wappingers Falls, another Franciscan, Father Frank Genevieve, is raping boys.

In the shadowed basement among statues of martyrs and coiled serpents, Masseo initiates new altar boys—some as young as eight—cajoling, grabbing, touching, encouraging, tearing at clothes, dropping the pants he wears under his robe to masturbate and more. In the sacristy, older boys make wagers: If a new boy spends half an hour alone with Masseo, he's "okay with it." Not every boy is molested. No one says anything. Nothing ever happens. Gifts and privileges flow for some. Others fear their parents' anger more than they fear Masseo's predations. Emboldened, Masseo appears in the school, pulling boys out of class to "carry candles" up to the church, hurrying them to the sacristy and then to the deserted basement.

I never serve a single Mass. I get into a tussle with Jackie Amadori, an older altar boy from Bond Street. Masseo, foul breath in my face, eyes bulging behind thick eyeglasses, rushes over and dismisses me with a slap. I feel like Adam banished from the Garden. I like to think I was bigger, smarter, savvier than the others, but I don't know what would have happened had I stayed.

Masseo is not alone. In Gowanus, there are solitary men—some innocent, like the old sailor who walks up Carroll Street with a parrot on his shoulder selling penny whistles and the Eastern European peddler going door-to-door hawking ribbons and cloth whom my mother refers to as "my Jew." Others pay to perform oral sex on street kids. Leo the Queer, frail and rumpled, who lives in a rancid-smelling apartment on Denton Place, drops dollars out his window the way fishermen chum bait. Friday nights, teens wanting beer money or ten dollars to take a girl to the RKO Prospect troop up to Leo's apartment. An open secret until it isn't.

At Mass, Father Arthur Lattanzi, our new pastor, rages

about Leo, a degenerate living next door to the church. He sends a posse of parishioners rushing to Leo's door, Masseo leading the charge. To me, it's the torch-wielding mob in *Frankenstein.* Meanwhile, two older altar boys are extorting hush money from Masseo, who steals the cash from the Sunday collection baskets, donations the nuns insist are for the "starving children of Africa."

A great inner-city exodus is underway: white flight spurred by racial fear, the myth of suburbia, the opening of the Verrazano Bridge. In the seventies, churches begin to empty, changing traditional Catholic education forever. In Brooklyn and Queens, 132 parochial schools shut their doors, Our Lady of Peace among them. There are no more altar boys.

In 1973, a gala celebrates Brother Masseo's fiftieth anniversary as a Franciscan. Bishops, priests, nuns, and laypeople gather to salute the man's "dedication, loving personality and warm heart . . . The memories carved in the hearts of all who were blessed to know him." Masseo Butteri dies in May 1979, a "humble giant of a man." (He was short.)

Forty years pass before the first lawsuit is filed, one of nearly six hundred sex abuse cases brought against the diocese of Brooklyn. It alleges Brother Masseo raped a seven-year-old boy in 1952. He was joined by another Franciscan, Father Rudolph Manozzi. They abused the little boy for years, sometimes in the second-floor boys' restroom where I first encountered Masseo. Allegedly, Masseo raped the child more than 125 times in the sacristy, a chapel, the school.

The story is confirmed by another Our Lady of Peace

altar boy, today a retired police officer, who was not abused. He remains anonymous because he has family still living in the neighborhood, and the old rules about never talking to strangers are still in force even if Gowanus no longer exists. Last I heard, the diocese is strenuously defending these cases. I'm told by one of two plaintiffs who've filed suit against Masseo that he suspects the church will dodge and delay until he dies. (In fact, they claim their insurance company is bankrupt.) In the winter of 2025, the woman who administers the parish's Facebook page—I grew up with her father—reminds me Masseo is "dead a hundred years. It's really none of my business nor anyone else's on this page!" The code of silence is very much in place. I sometimes wonder who decided there should be a passageway connecting the all-male rectory crowded with supposedly celibate men to an elementary school's boys' bathroom.

CHAPTER SIX

Vincenzo Coppola

Vincenzo is long dead, an unsmiling man with a thick accent who pinched my cheeks when I was a boy and made me cry. Vincenzo left his struggling family in Italy, lived for a time in Argentina where he was a *frutero,* a lowly fruit peddler. In Brooklyn, Anna Falcone, a talented seamstress from Pagani, Vincenzo's hometown, sees her marriage collapse, and her husband, an *impotente,* is sent packing. *Sensali* (matchmakers) get to work: Vincenzo, summoned, delivers (though he arrives with eight dollars to his name). He and Anna soon have five children, my father the only boy. When I'm older, Gloria whispers that Vincenzo cost my father and his sisters their inheritance. I'm not surprised. At that point, Vincenzo is chasing me and my cousin Stevie for trampling his garden or messing with his wine press.

✦ ✦ ✦

Within twenty years of arriving in Brooklyn, Anna and her sister, Alfonsina, known to me as La Zia (the Aunt), open a dressmaker's shop and a grocery and buy houses, including a six-story apartment building at 276 Third Avenue, the most valuable property in the neighborhood. There's a palazzo in Pagani, south of Naples, in the old country. As a kid, I fantasize about our Italian palace.

Anna dies in her forties, a decade before I'm born. Zia, homely as a witch in a fairy tale, decides that Vincenzo, handsome and strapping, should now marry her, a custom not unheard of among immigrants. Of course, he refuses, and bad blood flows across generations. After World War II, Zia sends Vincenzo, still her business partner, to Italy to collect rent on properties accruing since before the war. He sails off and doesn't return for a year.

According to INS records, Vincenzo arrives back in Brooklyn on the *Saturnia* on Christmas Eve 1950. Dead broke. Furious, Zia not only strips him of his portion—this simple fruit peddler!—but kicks my father and his four sisters out of her will. We wind up living next door to her in a run-down thirty-five-dollar-a-month apartment above a bar (also owned by Zia). Time passes. Resentment drips in our house like leaking pipes. One night when Zia's out of town, I'm doing my homework on the kitchen table. I hear this loud grunting and scraping coming from the hall staircase.

"What the hell?"

I open the door, peer down the darkened hall to the staircase where Sonny the Indian, Honey Christiano, and a third guy, his back to me, are muscling a steel safe down the stairs. When I catch Honey's eye, he nods toward our door, sending me back up the stairs.

"Jeez!"

I walk into the "parlor" of our three-room flat—my parents and brothers are watching *Paladin*—to tell my father.

"Don't pay no attention," he growls before I say a word.

Next day, I learn Zia's three-hundred-pound Diebold safe has vanished. For weeks, there's a smirk plastered on Uncle Honey's face. For the next decade, if I need a summer job, want a car, or if some punk is threatening me, Honey is there.

✦ ✦ ✦

When Zia dies, the estate goes to her son and a distant cousin, Mariuchelle, brought over from Italy. For the next twenty years, I walk past "our" apartment building damning my grandfather, *my* Italian palazzo now the stuff of fairy tales.

May 1981. A reporter, I'm part of a *Newsweek* team rushed to Rome to cover the attempted assassination of John Paul II, the Polish pope. Our bureau, on elegant Via dei Condotti, is a few yards from the Spanish Steps. For weeks, we chase a story as complex and twisty as a John le Carré thriller. I wind up in Ankara, Turkey, following a lead given me by an alleged Mossad asset in Tuscany. When I get back to Rome to file my story, Aunt Tessie, my father's older sister, is in Rome as a tourist. Tessie is fluent in Italian and, over the years, has stayed in contact with our family. She's just a phone call away.

"Why don't we visit?" I suggest.

Sunday morning, I rent a car and drive 135 miles south to Pagani. Tessie and I spend the afternoon with our relatives, the only time I ever meet them. The eldest is a medical doctor who lives with her husband, a French teacher named Aeneas Falcone, in a huge apartment that would have been grand one hundred years earlier. The living room wall, split by an earthquake, is unrepaired.

There's not much demand for French in a city where the spoken language sounds exactly like the guttural dialect I hear in Brooklyn, and the people are as loud and rough. I discover I'm part of the *intellighenzia* rather than a Brooklyn mope. Aeneas gives me a twelve-volume (!) history he's written of tiny Pagani. He pulls out a tattered, outsize book with a painstaking illustration of our family tree. The branches end abruptly with Anna and Zia's emigration early in the twentieth century. I fill in the blanks, making sure to include Vincenzo.

There follows the Sunday-afternoon feast with the Coppola relatives, the pasta and braciole, sausage, roast chicken, and stuffed artichokes, exactly like the Sunday-afternoon dinners I've eaten my whole life. These are people of modest means and I'm certain they've blown their weekly budget on our dinner.

I can't speak Italian, but the emotions are clear as a crystal stream. That morning, I didn't know these folk existed except as names passed down over the generations. Now we're embracing and laughing and trying to make each other understood. Word has spread that we're in town. Cousin after cousin, distant relatives, family friends show up carrying boxes of pastry, bottles of wine, and baskets of fruit, a story I hear again and again when Americans visit the old country. One guy is a double of my blond-haired brother, Thomas—mystery solved. After a while, the room begins to buzz. People are staring. A few pointing at me.

"Vincenzo Coppola e qui! Vincenzo Coppola e venuto!" (Vincent Coppola is here!)

Strangers hug me, some with tears in their eyes. At one point, a man in his forties comes up and embraces me. "I was a little boy, and I needed an operation," he says as Aunt Tessie translates. "Your grandfather, he paid for it."

And then a woman tells me Vincenzo gave her the money to open a beauty salon. And another whose tuition he'd paid, and another. He bought the food that kept these people from starving. A man assures me my grandfather tried to get him legal papers so he could emigrate to the United States. It didn't work out, but it's okay. He never forgot. No one ever forgot.

Vincenzo spent Zia's money on good works, on our family, far needier than their American counterparts. He dies, as many old Italians in Brooklyn do, of a heart attack working in his tiny garden. My strongest memory of him is this cranky old man pinching my cheeks until I cry. But that was not him. Not him at all. In my mind, I'd created a monster. He was an angel.

CHAPTER SEVEN

The Persimmon Tree

The tree, planted by my grandfather Vincenzo before I was born, dominates our yard. Green and vital, its limbs claw above the windowless brick-and-cinder-block walls that enclose us like a prison yard. It's a persimmon tree with shiny two-tone leaves and fissured bark like alligator hide. Trees are rare things in this part of Brooklyn. On Carroll Street, ours is the only house with a backyard tree. Johnny the Butcher has a pigeon coop; Joey DeSimone, rosebushes; Honey, a circular blue swimming pool. A few sickly ailanthus trees line the banks of the Gowanus; we strip the leaves and slash one another with the whiplike branches. To see real trees, I must walk six long blocks uphill to Prospect Park.

Vincenzo makes bad wine in our cellar. He twists my cheek between his thumb and forefinger—*"Come sie bello!"* (So handsome!)—until I scream. I hide rusty barrel hoops in his garden hoping he'll step on one. He coaxes tomatoes, peppers, melons, and squash from his tiny plot. Figs and grapes also blossom in Vincenzo's garden, but the persimmon tree is his pride and joy.

As long as Vincenzo lives, the tree never bears fruit. Not once. His obsession becomes mine. Year after year, I wait for spring, watch the tree flower, and never produce fruit. In biology class, I discover persimmon trees are gender-specific. Judging by its skimpy stamens and overripe pistils, this is a female though it can switch sex like the "morphadites" neighborhood men are always shouting about.

"What are you, a fucking morphadite?"

I walk to the Brooklyn Botanic Garden on Washington Avenue, a risky journey for a white high school kid in the early sixties. I'm told that—for a price—a botanist will show up with a ladder and pollinate our sixty-foot tree. I don't see this happening at my house.

When Vincenzo dies, my father inherits 474 Carroll Street and the persimmon tree in the backyard. Grapes grow, roses bloom, tomatoes ripen on vines. The persimmon tree remains barren. On spring evenings, I lie beneath its thick branches, counting the airliners flying overhead, imagining other places, other people, other worlds.

Time passes. Gowanus changes. At one point, under threat of a lawsuit brought by a yuppie tenant worried about her toddler playing in the yard, I have Vincenzo's magical dirt analyzed by an environmental expert at Syracuse University. She basically tells me there's enough lead and base metal in the soil to build a chemical weapon.

"So I'm screwed?"

"Maybe not," the scientist says. "All the yards in South Brooklyn are toxic."

◆ ◆ ◆

A wiseguy buys the house next door, a gift for his mother who's grown restless living in a Long Island mansion and misses Gowanus. Her friends are here. He orders a ground-up restoration, no expense spared, though he's not paying retail. Workers disassemble the place brick by brick, then painstakingly put it back together installing imported marble and tile, state-of-the-art HVAC systems, and a designer kitchen. Gloria tells me that during the yearlong restoration, dubious Bell System phone "workers" and Con Edison "crews" continually try to gain entry to our cellar. Of course, she chases them away. We're gifted a turkey on Thanksgiving Day in gratitude.

Ceilings are raised, the cellar lowered. An African American craftsman arrives from "down south" to hand-carve moldings and banisters. The exterior, a modernist take on a Victorian brownstone, enormous oval glass windows set like eyes in the facade. The actor James Caan—the wiseguy is godfather to Caan's son Scott—donates the bronze lion's head knocker that stares balefully through wrought-iron bars onto the sidewalk. In the backyard, a gazebo sprouts. Our rusty chain-link fence is replaced by a pink-brick wall, topped by a sinuous curve. In effect, they have built a Venetian palace across the street from Monte's "Venetian Room."

◆ ◆ ◆

In the mid-eighties, our family blows apart. My brother Thomas dies of AIDS, his chiseled body and handsome features so disfigured I can't recognize him. My brother Joe is shooting heroin. Gloria's throat cancer has returned. My father, a nonstop smoker, develops full-blown emphysema. Another sibling is on the run from gangsters—he's run up enormous gambling debts. Determined to find him, they track me down in Hanoi, where I'm on a magazine assignment.

I still make my way to the backyard to sit among the dozen rosebushes I've planted in Thomas's memory. Many years after Vincenzo's passing, the cinder-block walls are covered in lush green moss like an enclosed English garden. The persimmon towers above all, branches thick with glistening leaves that overhang the adjoining yards like a canopy.

One day, I arrive to find the house deathly silent. My father, a shadow of the tough-as-nails longshoreman I loved and feared, sits drowsing on the plastic-covered living room couch, an oxygen mask covering half his face. The machine hisses and gurgles, a sound I hate. I walk through the kitchen, pull open the back door, and step into the yard.

I stand there astonished.

All that remains of the persimmon tree is a blunt, blackened stump, its amputated branches reaching to the heavens in shame and supplication. Everything, save for a carpet of rotting leaves, is gone. Thomas's rose garden has been crushed by falling branches. Tears stream down my checks. I charge back inside.

"Daddy, what's happened! Who did this to our tree! Who the fuck did this?"

He looks at me. I notice he's crying behind the mask.

"The lady next door complained the leaves were falling in her yard."

"Falling in her yard, so you cut Grandpa's tree down?"

"I wouldn't do that. Honey sent a crew of guys with chain saws. I couldn't stop them." In the past, my father would have sent them running.

I stand there enraged and suddenly impotent. An old lady picks up her phone and complains about dead leaves in her yard—probably happens a thousand times a day in America, but in Gowanus her wish is somebody's command. And seventy-five years of family history—my grandfather, my brother Thomas who'd bring Easter rabbits and ducks on the subway to live under the tree, the July Fourth barbecues, rosebushes and tomato plants, our joys and tragedies—vanish.

CHAPTER EIGHT

Golten's Yard

At night, I listen to the low groan of foghorns in the upper harbor, and the relentless clanking of a behemoth echoing across our backyards, an overhead crane lifting marine boilers and diesel engines the size of freight cars.

Golten's Yard runs like a spine from Third Avenue to the Gowanus Canal, ribbed by dilapidated row houses on one side and, on the other, Golten Marine, a WWII-era ship-repair operation, an artifact of a Brooklyn peopled by Norwegians and Germans who settled here years before my great-grandfather and his seven sons arrived on the canal. In other words (at least to me), the beginning of time.

The rusting carcasses of ship engines are scattered everywhere and superstructures loom like skeletal dinosaurs over my head. There are propulsion and navigation panels with needle dials and brass levers out of *Twenty Thousand Leagues Under the Sea,* antiquated electrical transformers, acres of pipes, enormous spools of cable.

The city's Gowanus playground is a few blocks away, at

Nevins and Douglass Streets, but its kiddie pool is clogged with trash and nodding junkies roost on its wooden benches. Prospect Park—Olmsted and Vaux's "other" great New York City park, with its rolling hills and sparkling meadows—is less than a mile away, but it might as well be Yellowstone. And neighboring Red Hook, just on the other side of the Brooklyn–Queens Expressway, and its tribalized Puerto Ricans, the Amazon.

Ghosts are everywhere in this part of Brooklyn. Momentous events, vague history, and restless spirits hover just beyond my ken. Seventeenth-century Dutch farmers built dikes and millponds on a saltwater estuary a half mile from my house. In August 1776, 259 Marylanders died shielding George Washington's retreating Continental Army in the Old Stone House on Third Street, where I play softball on a field glittering with broken glass. Edwin Litchfield, a nineteenth-century developer, carved the estuary into a bustling commercial waterway lined by gasworks, factories, coal yards, docks, and slaughterhouses, triggering the monumental pollution that defines Gowanus. I know nothing of these things.

I have Golten's Yard, a Coney Island of thrills, danger, and mischief—admission via a hole in the fence in Honey Christiano's backyard. After school, on weekends, in summer and winter, we disappear, like Alice in *Through the Looking-Glass,* into a world where there are no adults, no rules, no cops, and certainly no safety nets. A three-room shack on Third Avenue is a fort we assault and defend with homemade slingshots firing extruded rubber pellets that litter the ground, and when out of those, rocks and bolts. Bleeding and exhausted, we collapse to the ground.

I crawl over the machines searching for swag JuJu, Robert Schiano, and Jimmy Psycho steal from freight depots and warehouses alongside the canal. This is a Gowanus tradition going back half a century. Once I find a box of Italian leather handbags before *i mariuoli* (the thieves) can fence it. (Gloria loves her Mother's Day present.)

One Sunday morning, FBI agents confront us, guns drawn, as we stand, astounded, before a fifteen-foot-tall tower of cases of Del Monte pineapple juice. They're hunting a legendary gang of hijackers—"the Forty Thieves"—allegedly started decades earlier by Al Capone. But all they bag is a ragged crew of fifteen-year-olds.

A kick in the ass and we're gone.

The day comes when Golten Marine shuts down. The overhead crane haunting my dreams goes silent. A watchman is left behind to look after the premises—a gray wooden structure, eighty yards long, walls lined with hundreds of small windowpanes. So many, it takes me months to break them. After school, I slip into the yard alone, climb a hill of scrap metal, and sail rocks through windows, methodically working my way up like Sisyphus. I don't know why I do this. I do imagine other boys playing baseball, studying, taking guitar lessons from Buddy Sanfratello on Henry Street, walking girls home from school.

Weeks later, the watchman, who speaks what I imagine is German, strikes back, hooking up a scratchy recording—machine-gun fire, bombs bursting, shouts, and screams—to the foundry's powerful PA system and blasts me off my perch. When he finally quits, Golten's is defenseless; like Visigoths sacking Rome, packs of teens from other neighborhoods descend, smashing, trashing, wilding. I ignore them and spend days blistering my hands as I systematically drive a V-shaped steel beam—balanced on a horizontal cement-filled barrel—along the bottom of a masonry wall. When the structure collapses, I barely avoid being crushed. Victory.

Hubba-Hubba, a prince of the Barbella clan, ties a thick mooring line to the bottom of the overhead crane, adds a short wooden board for a seat, and soon we're leaping from the catwalk and sailing twenty feet above the rubble-covered concrete floor on a super swing—until it snaps, and Joey Romano, a troublemaker who extorts exam answers from me in elementary school, breaks his arm. Thirty years later, Joey is found shot to death wrapped in a rug in the trunk of a car on Van Brunt Street. The murder is still unsolved.

Before the other marauders arrive, Sal, Ernie, and I break into Golten's laboratory. There, we discover rows of gleaming beakers, test tubes, pipettes, sulfuric and hydrochloric acids, scores of chemicals in brown glass bottles. We grab what we can and hide our stash in the back of an abandoned truck in the yard for "research." Or something.

A budding scientist who mixes medicine cabinet potions on our windowsill, I decide to buy gas masks for our experiments. Crossing Flatbush Avenue, heading for the army and navy store adjacent to Buddy Lee's men's shop ("Where style begins"), I'm hit by a taxi. My front teeth are knocked out and my left knee smashed.

Soon I'm back in Golten's cellar hunting more treasure.

By now, the power has been cut off, so we roll newspapers into torches, illumination enough to reveal we're ankle-deep in shit from the shattered toilets.

"Screw this!" I toss my torch and head up the stairs. Anyway, it's lunchtime.

Half an hour later, I'm sitting in Gloria's kitchen eating a salami sandwich leaking Gulden's mustard. Sirens wail in the distance, grow louder, and crescendo in a piercing scream. Fire trucks race along Third Avenue, past Carroll, then . . . silence.

"Jesus!" Gloria exclaims.

Stomach churning, I get up from the table, walk to the front door, pull it open, and look outside. A crowd is gathered on the corner, the air pungent with acrid black smoke.

"Fuck!"

Golten Marine is ablaze. Flames soar one hundred feet in the air. Firemen race to hook up hoses. They break through the overhead door into a Niagara of fire, and they search for workers possibly trapped inside.

I've burned down Golten's Yard.

CHAPTER NINE

A Summer in Paradise

Carroll Street is teeming, the air thick with humidity and fumes belched from trucks thundering along Third Avenue. Gamblers, Jerry Pepe, Freddie Fish, Muzzi among them, stand on the corner shouting, cursing, scratching their balls, arguing the afternoon card at Aqueduct. Across the street by the Capri Club, Mikey Romanelli and the Goose, dressed like undertakers in dark suits, hover, collecting bets, and, later, losers. The scribbled sheets are stored in the blue US post office mailbox next to the red fire alarm box on the corner, a safe place since no one trusts the post office after Americo Guzzi dropped a cherry bomb down the chute.

Next door, Chitty and Buffalo Manzo grill steaks and sausage in a charcoal-filled drum, slathered with peppers and onions and served on bread from Gallo's Bakery, the intoxicating aroma wafting in the air. On the other corner, ancient Rosina ("Ru-zeen") churns lemon ice for truckers lined up in front of her store for a dime's worth scooped into a Dixie cup. At night, she hangs a naked bulb above the side door of the grocery and fries ten-cent calzones in a sizzling vat of burned oil while you wait. Rosina is missing the tip of one of her fingers and the "surprise" kids look for is finding the digit in your calzone.

Farther along Third toward First Street, there's a clanging as Victor the Blacksmith, biceps bulging in a medieval-looking leather vest, shoes horses for Jumbo Angioletti and the fruit peddlers who'll sing out in Italian from their horse and wagons, "*E rook e' rob,*" (broccoli rabe), another smell in the air, another sound adding to the cacophony. A one-eyed rooster who's lost track of time struts and frets all day in front of Goldie's Live Poultry Market.

This is my world. I wander its streets oblivious to the fact that I don't live, as my grandparents did, in the shadow of Vesuvius. In the sixties, Gowanus is a peculiar place, an artifact of the Mezzogiorno, of southern Italy, all its joys and ills, dropped in the middle of New York City.

Singsong, girls skip rope, play hopscotch on boxes chalked in pastels on the cracked sidewalk. I shout and curse, pitch pennies in front of John Sanseverino's candy store, play kings against the wall of the Typhoon Air Conditioning Co. and occasionally high-stakes stickball when the Goose pits his "Seven Battlers" against squads from other neighborhoods on Sunday mornings. No one cares that the crumbling brick wall running along First Street from Third Avenue is a remnant of Washington Park, Brooklyn's first professional baseball stadium. Should a fly ball soar over your head, keep running. Goose is a sore loser.

Church bells sing out the Angelus; Carvel trucks blast their maddening jingles. Fat Rosie, Baby Doll, Baby Chick, and the *maldicenza* ("mad-un-geens") sit outside sweltering apartments, gossiping and knitting beaded hats like Madame Defarge before the guillotine, never missing a thing.

Sweltering, we have no pools, no sprinklers, no garden hoses. A visit to the public pool in Red Hook means battling Puerto Ricans and Blacks from the Gowanus projects who name themselves "Untouchable Bishops" and "Apaches." Instead, we open the johnny pump next to Monte's, grab a twenty-eight-ounce can of Italian tomatoes—top and bottom removed—squat down behind the gushing hydrant, hands cupped tightly around the can, and send a powerful spout of water jetting thirty to forty feet in the air onto the far sidewalk. Instantly, younger kids are in bathing suits, teenage girls wriggle in shorts and suddenly see-through blouses, and the guys are knocked on their asses by frigid blasts.

We wait (this is who we are) for the convertible Electra 225s and Caddies driven by wiseguys in leisure suits to cross the Carroll Street Bridge from Court and Henry Streets. They slow to a crawl, pull cigars from their mouths, shoot warnings, then murderous looks, assuming we know better. We fucking drown them and dart into the empty lots behind our houses.

Fat Ernie backs his four-door '56 Oldsmobile up to a gushing hydrant on Third Street and Bond, slides down the rear power window. I'm in the back seat with three other guys when a tsunami roars through the open window, knocking me senseless. I'm underwater, drowning, panicking, fighting to open the door in a moving car on

Union Street in the middle of May. Ernie relents, and we're gushed like sewage into the gutter a block from the Gowanus.

✦ ✦ ✦

Saturdays, my brother Thomas and I climb the creaky wooden steps to the top floor of our row house. Up the ladder, through the hatch, onto the sticky tar roof. We spread towels, eat salami sandwiches, sun ourselves, read novels. To the north, Manhattan's towers beckon like the Hindu Kush. Unspoken, we're both planning to summit these heights.

✦ ✦ ✦

Weeks before the Fourth of July, skirmishes begin, leading up to cataclysmic war. Fireworks flow into the neighborhood from Chinatown where you can buy a five-dollar mat from "Chinks" on Canal Street or Italians in loud shirts on Mott Street (they mug you before you get back to the subway station). Wiseguys import truckloads from North Carolina; each day the explosions are more prolonged and intense. Firecrackers give way to cherry bombs, torpedoes, ash cans, M-80s, rockets, helicopters, whistling "nigga-chasers" that race along the sidewalk before exploding.

On July 4, Honey Christiano combines all the unsold fireworks into a daylong explosion fest. In all things, wiseguys are like murderous children: fun to them is throwing a braided pack of exploding firecrackers in your face, a powerful ash can into your car, aiming a blazing Roman candle through an open window. Americo Guzzi's father, who once threw a kitten from his third-floor window, takes a retaliatory fireball in the head. By three p.m., Carroll Street is ankle-deep in exploded fireworks. Little boys hunt for unexploded ordnance, blowing off their fingertips. My ears ring for hours.

Nightfall sends barrages of rockets into the overheated air. Buffalo takes a sizzling bottle rocket in the eye. Partially blinded, he'll be ready next year. Honey, master thief, somehow locates mortars destined for the Coney Island fireworks show where they're to be set off on an offshore barge. He ignites them on the corner of Third Avenue and Carroll. No one is killed. He produces military flare guns and fires multicolored exploding cartridges on parachutes onto our tar paper roofs.

June 1962. I'm fourteen, getting ready for the Fourth, when Gloria announces that Joe, my uncle Sonny Boy Giordano, and my muscle-bound police lieutenant cousin Johnny Pomarico are buying a summer place in the Catskills. She says it's "Paradise Park." I can still feel the grin spread across my face. This doesn't happen in my life. I've read about Rip Van Winkle, but I've never been north of Manhattan, and only then with a robed parochial school nun.

Paradise Park?

We pile into Joe's '56 mint-green Coupe de Ville, vast trunk loaded with suitcases, sheets, towels, toiletries, toys, Wiffle balls, boxes of pasta, cans of peeled tomatoes, coolers packed with Genoa salami, "gabagool," ravioli, sausages, roasted peppers, hunks of Parmigiano, and creamy mozzarella. All eyes on us—no one leaves Gowanus for vacation—as Joe pulls away like the *Queen Elizabeth* leaving her berth. A right turn on Third Avenue—I half wave to Chitty and Buffalo—then a mile to Hamilton Avenue and onto the Brooklyn–Battery Tunnel.

Condensation on the curved walls, the hiss of pressurized air and roar of the huge ventilation fans convince me I'm underwater, and collapse is imminent. Then we're on the West Side Highway, where a Yale tractor trailer sits atop a building on West 39th Street, the mannequin driver smiling at me.

Northward bound.

✦ ✦ ✦

Three hours later, Joe, chain-smoking, frazzled, cursing, slaps wildly at Joey and Thomas carousing in the back seat. I sit behind him out of range. Gloria, Gregory in her lap, is trying to avoid the cataclysmic crash I know is imminent. Suddenly, the sky opens: 23A, a two-lane state road, becomes a series of curves and switchbacks hugging a forested mountain. We pass a gushing waterfall, a moment so unexpected and overpowering we fall silent.

✦ ✦ ✦

Tannersville. On Spring Street, houses have names like "Dingle Dell" and "Apple Drop." A mile up the road, I spot a splintery wooden sign, *Paradise Park* painted in fat yellow letters. Joe turns left into a driveway, one side lined with droopy fir trees; the other, a cottage with a bearded Orthodox Jew standing by the door. At the end of the driveway, there's a white shingled house with green trim and a big front porch. Half a dozen cars are parked haphazardly.

I stumble out of the back seat and stretch, the familiar smell of simmering sauce punctuating the mountain air. Ten of my cousins come whooping and hollering out of nowhere, followed by my uncles Sonny Boy, Alley-Bo, Big Sonny, and aunts Babe, Marguerite, and Madeline, laughing, shouting, hugging, unfazed by the neighbor glaring through his kitchen window.

Cousin Lorraine grabs my arm; Louise runs up to Thomas and pulls him away.

"Come look!"

I spot a few crab apple trees, a patch of lawn, a stand of oak and pine, a second bungalow hanging over a creek; no way anyone will mistake this "paradise" for Bob Dylan's "home across the road." Over the next three summers Paradise Park will change my life. I can breathe, but it's new people and experiences more than mountain air.

Shmuel, the Orthodox Jew, rents the small bungalow with his teenage daughters, Claire and Berenice. Aunt Babe takes me with her when she walks over to turn off the lights, "Shabbos goy" meaningless to either of us. In Brooklyn, I think two Hasidim are the cough-drop-making Smith Brothers. His daughters are cute, though, to my practiced eye, unfashionable. Shmuel, a holdover in a mass exodus as the "Jewish Alps" give way to Miami Beach as the vacation spot of choice, politely refuses bowls of ravioli and sausage Gloria insists on sending him. He's gone when the lease runs out.

I have no problem meeting the locals; my female cousins are not shy. Soon enough, I run into a few guys loitering in the creek. After some skipping rocks and boy shit, Meigs, their freckled blond leader, plucks a frog off a rock.

"Look at this," he says and snaps a reed from the bank.

He shoves the reed up the frog's ass and blows, once, twice. The creature inflates, and Meigs sends it floating downstream.

"What the fuck!"

That's not the end of it. My cousin Clemmie, by far the best-looking girl in Our Lady of Peace School, marries this mope.

⬥ ⬥ ⬥

Tannersville calls itself the "Painted Village in the Sky," elevation all of 1,900 feet, about a third as high as Vermont's peaks. (Hunter, the next town, is building a ski lift.) Clemmie tells me that on Friday nights, Lake Rip Van Winkle is *the* place. I plan my debut carefully, shave my sideburns to the tops of my ears, don tight-fitting "casino" pants split at the cuffs, an orange pullover "poncho" shirt, pointed back and front, and matching orange socks (my turquoise outfit is too bold). I check the bathroom mirror before I walk the mile to the lake house.

"Shit!"

Two inches of fish belly white skin stare back. A quick application of Coney Island suntan—baby oil and iodine—and I'm off. It's dusk but still hot, and Spring Street is hilly. In five minutes, viscous orange liquid is oozing down my collar, my armpits soaked with sweat. I hurry by families relaxing on screened-in porches.

"Jesus, will you look at this idiot!" a man mutters.

A chorus of laughs. Another at the next house.

I hit Main Street, wait for nightfall, and hurry back to Paradise Park.

A week later at the lake house, I defeat the local checkers champion twice in a row, but what I remember is a girl named Paresi from Little Italy, squeezing my shoulder during the game. Clemmie, Miss Popularity, is friends with three blond sisters who sneak into the creek bungalow and hide cigarettes under my pillow. Shy, I ignore them but fall in love with the bookmobile lady who pulls into our driveway once a week. Sitting under the apple tree, I devour everything she picks out for me.

My family beats the town's softball team. In Brooklyn, my home-run-blasting cousin Jimmy Pomarico is so talented pro baseball scouts are courting him. Abandoned by his "whoremaster" (per Gloria) father and wanting security, Jimmy becomes a cop. My godfather "Blubberhead" Barbella is such a bust, I name Jimmy my godfather.

In Gowanus, I share these stories with Fat Ernie, Eggplant, Lenny Spares, and the rest of my friends. It's like I've been living in a Beach Boys song ("Two girls for every boy!") only in the run-down Catskills. The following spring, eight of us ride the Trailways bus to Tannersville. I have the keys to Paradise Park. We arrive on a Friday night so revved up we walk to the lake house. It's pitch-dark, off-season, the place is shuttered, but someone has noticed us.

Walking back up South Main Street—there are no sidewalks—headlights flare, engines roar, tires burn rubber as half a dozen cars, my cousin Clemmie's frog-ass-blowing boyfriend's red Ford Galaxie convertible in the lead, charge, horns blowing, run us off the road and into a muddy ditch.

CHAPTER TEN

The Outsider

"*Ue mammone!*" one of the guys standing outside the Capri Club shouts as Joe Tramontano crosses Third Avenue. He's a grown man, but he's pulling a child's red wagon piled with books. My friends laugh, I look away. The wagon bumps over the curb, and the man continues down the block.

"*Ue mammone!*"

He pronounces it "way-ma-moan," each syllable hanging in the air like ragged underwear on a clothesline. In this world, mockery is a constant: singsong, aural graffiti, echoing everywhere. *Mammone* is "mama's boy," but it cuts deeper. A *mammone* is incompetent, incapable, absurd. Tramontano, my college-educated cousin, my imagined connection to the larger world, is a laughingstock. A walking metaphor for the mistrust of education, of books, and those who read books, of politicians, outsiders, priests, authority, a stream flowing back to the poverty and cynicism of the Mezzogiorno, our wellspring.

My father and uncles, almost all dockworkers, joke that

everything I know "is out of books." (I think, therefore I don't exist?) The teasing is affectionate, even protective. I'm trying to make sense of the world.

Joseph Tramontano is another story, a self-proclaimed Marxist, rabble-rouser, revolutionary among the wiseguys, fruit peddlers, laborers, gamblers on the corner. At Zia's apartment—we live next door—he works on brainteasers in *Scientific American* magazine or fiddles with a ham radio, an unheard-of technology. The medium of choice in Gowanus is the homing pigeon. On Third Avenue, a gaggle of aficionados, serious as thoroughbred breeders, gather to gamble, gossip, and breed the birds like Brando in *On the Waterfront*. My brother Thomas has my father build him a coop. In the most shameful act of my life, I shoot one of Johnny the Butcher's prized birds with a Marlin .22 target rifle my father buys me for my birthday.

Neighborhood girls ride the RR and F trains into lower Manhattan to dead-end clerical, sales, and factory jobs in the jumble of streets around Washington Square Park. A hotbed of labor unrest even before the 1911 Triangle Shirtwaist Factory fire killed 146 workers, most of them women. The Gowanus girls complain about the bug-eyed, spittle-spraying *stronzo* (shithead), calling them by name on their lunch breaks with mad talk of socialism and revolution.

At communal family meals, my oft-pregnant mother watches Joe shovel spaghetti, ravioli, steaming bowls of minestra, beef, and veal braciole down his throat, declaring he's entitled to extra food to "feed his brain." My father is unloading freighters on the Black Diamond

Lines' piers to make the thirty-five-dollar monthly rent Zia Alfonsina charges him.

✦ ✦ ✦

Alfonsina hires a piano teacher to give Tramontano lessons. She imports Mariuchelle (Little Mary), a cousin from Italy, to keep him company. For my cousins and me, his origin story is a mystery.

Time passes. Tramontano's études float across the hallway to our apartment where Gloria serves *pasta e pizzelle,* peas and pasta, three times a week. Tramontano becomes a repairer of typewriters and printing presses, then a pharmacist, the Marxist revolution apparently on hold. He marries. And remarries. It's a blur in my adolescent mind.

✦ ✦ ✦

My grandparents' generation is passing away, and with it, the connections and rituals I so love: Easter mornings at Holy Cross Cemetery when the dead are again part of the family; my uncle Sonny Boy, an NYPD sergeant singing at raucous "football weddings" while rye whiskey flows and "gabagool" (capicola) sandwiches ricochet from table to table; Sunday mornings, Grandmother Clementina Giordano bent over a cast iron frying pan, handing out sizzling meatballs on forks to half a dozen eager grandchildren; Vincenzo Coppola's tomato plants flourishing among the weeds and broken glass in the backyard.

Bonds are shredding. Records, once painstakingly kept in longhand, become slipshod, memories unravel. Tramontano relocates to Staten Island, a subway and a five-cent ferry ride from Union Square. A third marriage is to the widowed mother of "Mikey the Jap," one of my bucktoothed classmates. In these years, Zia Alfonsina, nominally head of the Coppola clan, after nursing a lifetime of grudges, has cut my grandfather, my father, and my four aunts out of her will. She names Joe Tramontano and Mariuchelle heirs.

We live at 294 Third Avenue, above a bar and grill Zia owns. During Prohibition, not one to miss an opportunity, she ran a flexible pipe from the bar across four backyards to a wine press she'd secreted in the cellar of 474 Carroll Street, my grandfather Vincenzo the winemaker. A Y-shaped staircase leads to two second-floor apartments. Zia's sprawling flat is to the right at the end of a long hall. We're on the left, five of us shoehorned into three rooms. A bulky washing machine squats in our kitchen, a clothesline runs from our bathroom window across the backyards to the roof of Goldie's Live Poultry Market.

A door constructed of heavy wood and rectangular glass panes sits at a right angle to Zia's apartment. It fascinates me. It's always locked. When pale light glimmers behind its frosted glass, I scoot up to the roof, count skylights covered in pigeon shit until I'm standing above the locked door. The skylight won't budge. Back downstairs, I press my face against the glass. The room behind the door is named *stanzina*, an unfamiliar word.

Zia, now widowed, lives with Nunzio, an elderly Italian man—wattled chin and bald pate freckled with liver spots—who dresses fastidiously in suit, tie, and pearl stickpin. Both are in their eighties. To me, Zia, with her hawk nose, bulging eyes, and drooping flesh, is the Evil Queen in *Snow White.* Nunzio is a gentle man who naps a lot. His dresser contains things to tempt me—folding knives, Italian lira, Indian-head pennies, dentures, a wind-up pocket watch.

I'm obsessed with the *stanzina.* Nunzio translates the word as "little room." Every day after school, I fly up the staircase, take the right fork, hurry down the hall, and rattle the doorknob. Locked. Locked. Exasperated, Nunzio tells me Tramontano has the only key. One afternoon, while Zia and Nunzio nap, I fiddle with the lock using my father's screwdriver. After ten minutes, a metallic click. Catching my breath, I turn the knob and pull. Under the grime-flecked skylight are dusty glass bookcases filled with rows and rows of hardcover books, science, philosophy, history, politics, art, religion, literature. Magazines, mostly *Life* and *Time,* but also the *Daily Worker, American Socialist,* and "dirty magazines," like *SPAN* and *Stare,* are piled on the floor.

A library. I read paperbacks from the Fourth Avenue newsstand. This is a miracle. It's as if one of the great libraries of antiquity has materialized twenty feet from my door. There are photo albums sealed in plastic and labeled in small, neat print. In one curious photo, a much younger Tramontano, in a zoot suit, stands grinning next my father and Blubberhead, my godfather, next to a 1940 Buick convertible.

I jam a wooden matchstick into the latch mechanism. Over the next month, I ferry books in and out of the shadowed room. Of course, I grab *Stare,* but also *Oliver Twist* from a bound collection of Charles Dickens's works. In other bookcases, I find *Huckleberry Finn, For Whom the Bell Tolls, A Farewell to Arms, The War of the Worlds, The Grapes of Wrath*, *The Time Machine*, *The Canterbury Tales*. The illustrated jackets of *Das Kapital* and *Mein Kampf* tempt me, but they're unreadable.

One winter afternoon, thumbing through a stack of *Life* magazines, I come across "At the Gates of Hell: The Liberation of Bergen-Belsen, April 1945." I don't know the word for what I'm seeing, but I'm paralyzed, terrified, mesmerized, ripped from the overheated little room and dropped among gas chambers, rotting corpses, acres of shoes, hanks of hair, dresses, striped prison uniforms, a child's rag doll. My eyes race to decipher the next obscenity and thus shield my brain. I stagger out, down the long hallway, and up the short flight of stairs to our apartment. Gloria is frying eggplant, the most ordinary thing in the world.

I avoid the *stanzina* for weeks.

This time, when I press her, Gloria says Zia Alfonsina, visiting our family in Pagani after World War II, carried young Tramontano back with her to Brooklyn. A Holocaust survivor. A Jew. Of course he is! That explains everything, every quirky, bizarre, or noble behavior. The intellectual. The radical. The outsider who never fit in. *Un mammone*. I understand.

I accept this story for the next forty years. In fact, when I arrive at Brooklyn College in the mid-sixties, I embellish it: Tramontano as Che Guevara, Joe Hill, Cesar Chavez, the *mammone* as hero. Books are cool. I pore over *Ramparts* magazine the way he must have studied *American Socialist*.

By then, Tramontano is dead, and our family has scattered. Why should it matter? Life goes on, right?

But the story isn't true.

In 2023, Joe Enright, a high school classmate with access to a trove of online census and other records, sends me a note.

Vinny,

Per the 1930 census info I sent you last night, Tramontano was living on Carroll Street with his parents a year before Hitler came to power.

He was born in Brooklyn.

CHAPTER ELEVEN

Eyes Closed Tight

On a winter afternoon, I'm crossing Third Avenue with my cousin Clementine when the ground trembles and a powerful gust scatters us like bowling pins. My tan schoolbag skitters across the pavement. A moment later, I'm deafened by a terrible roar. Cars, trucks, the B37 bus—frightened faces pressed against its windows—slam to a halt. Around us, Tony the Barber, Chitty the Fruit Peddler, Molly the Barkeep, Goose the Bookie are all mouthing words and pointing toward a pillar of smoke and flame rising in the west, but I can't hear a thing. We get to our feet as Gloria, Aunt Dolly, and other mothers pour out of the row houses. A fire truck races along Third Avenue, eerily silent to my deaf ears.

An atom bomb has hit Brooklyn, I think. I'm not scared, just sad. A sad parochial schoolboy at a moment when nuclear war with "godless Russia" is very close. A year before, Sister Mary Killian shared the miracle of Our Lady of Fatima: how the Blessed Virgin, "shining brighter than the sun," appeared to three young shepherds in

Portugal. Mary gives them three letters. I will be obsessed with these letters for the next twenty years. At first, I'm just curious.

What do they feel like?

Are they typed or written in longhand?

On parchment? Stationery?

Are there watermarks?

Latin? English? Portuguese?

No one answers these obvious questions. Then there are the contents: The first letter prophesied the end of World War I. The second, the beginning of WWII. The third letter? Killian says Pope Pius XII took a peek and fell to the ground, whether in terror or joy, she cannot say. He's going to reveal its contents any day. She proclaims this a miracle? I bemoan the end of the world. (Years later, Pat Gleason, my high school history teacher, tells me the third letter is the "bill for the Last Supper.") Like Jesus and Mary, I'm still a virgin. A few weeks before, images of Soviet tanks rolling into Budapest, crushing "freedom fighters," crowded our black-and-white TV screen. I have no idea where Hungary is, but I'm troubled. At Our Lady of Peace School, orange-and-black air raid instructions—distributed by Con Edison—stare at me from classroom walls (I steal one for my bedroom). We have regular air raid drills. Nuns in brown and black shrouds shout, "Under your desks! Cover exposed parts of your body! Close eyes tightly!"

Standing outside the barbershop, I watch stunned workers from Eagle Clothing and other factories stream along Third toward Atlantic Avenue, some bleeding, clothes torn, covered in grime and soot. And then a countermovement: my father, my cousin Jerry Pepe, my uncle Big Sonny Giordano, Mike the Geep, and other longshoremen rushing in the opposite direction toward the explosion.

How brave they are.

They're headed for Bush Terminal's 35th Street pier two miles away. In the sixties, Bush Terminal is the largest warehousing, manufacturing, and shipping complex in the country. As a child, I'd strain to read the enormous painted letters on a sign—think a Brobdingnagian eye chart—facing the Gowanus Expressway as we'd sail past in my father's green '56 Caddy on our way to Coney Island to watch Tuesday-night fireworks.

A Great Industrial City Within a City
Owned & Operated By
Bush Terminal Buildings Co.
Over 6 Million Sq. Ft.
Of Industrial Floor Space

Dockworkers were using an oxyacetylene torch to cut away a steel pillar to repair a cargo crane when the torch's six-thousand-degree heat ignited piles of burlap bags filled with foam rubber scrap. Armed only with handheld extinguishers, the longshoremen were driven back by billowing smoke and flame. As the fire trucks arrive, burning rubber—scattered on the pier like a trail of birdseed—ignites thirty-seven thousand pounds of *cordeau détonant,* detonating fuse, which no one realizes is there.

The blast—up to this point, the most powerful explosion in New York City history—rattles buildings across the East River on Wall Street, kills ten people, injures hundreds, shatters windows more than a mile away. So powerful, flying glass and metal shrapnel kill some unlucky soul half a mile away. The full force of the explosion on the elevated pier passes over the heads of firefighters on four FDNY boats racing across the upper harbor to combat what they mistake for a simple dockside fire.

That night, I race to the newsstand on Fourth Avenue and grab five-cent copies of the late editions of the *Daily News* and the *Daily Mirror*, the only papers—except for the *Morning Telegraph*—that ever appear in our house. Arriving home, I find Joe, Uncle Big Sonny, Cousin Jerry Pepe, and two other dockworkers in our backyard. They're sitting at the picnic table, downing Four Roses whiskey.

Joe Coppola is no drinker.

"Dad, I got the paper! The explosion is everywhere!"

"Go back in the house," he growls. "You don't need to see this."

Disappointed, I pass through the dented screen door into our narrow kitchen, past the sloshing washing machine.

"Mom, what are they doing?"

"Never mind. Go upstairs with your brothers."

"Mom—"

"Go." She turns back to the wash. Gloria wears makeup doing laundry.

I pound up the narrow, enclosed staircase my father jerry-rigged to connect the floors, claustrophobic as Queequeg's coffin. Pushing Joey and Tommy out of the way, I duck into my narrow room, a mirror image of the downstairs kitchen, and I close the door behind me. My window faces the backyard. I kneel, then carefully slide the sash open, ease my elbows above the whistling radiator onto the rusting fire escape. Trembling, I peer into the yard.

Under a naked light bulb strung from the grape trellis, the men are gathered around a wooden bench, the empty whiskey bottle on the table. Uncle Sonny straddles it, his right leg bent sideways at the knee. There's a folded washcloth in his hand. He removes his glasses, folds them, and puts them in his shirt pocket.

Two guys grasp him by the shoulders. Cousin Jerry is holding a short wooden-handled hammer.

"You ready?" Jerry asks. A thin, hyperactive man, an inveterate horseplayer, and usually the butt of my uncle Sonny's jokes and insults, Jerry never talks below a shout.

"Get going!" Sonny orders, stuffing the washcloth into his mouth.

Jerry stands there. Upstairs, I close my eyes tightly. I can't bear this.

"Fuck this! I ain't doing it!" Jerry says and steps away. He hands the hammer to my father. Joe steps forward and swings the hammer in a short, vicious arc. Sonny screams; the burly men hold him in place. After a moment, he nods.

My father hits him again.

I watch the men take turns smashing each other's knees with the bloody hammer, muffled moans driving me back into my dark room. These men are so much a part of my childhood. Uncle Sonny and Cousin Jerry show up at our house every Saturday morning during the racing season, usually joined by my uncle Sal Giordano, an NYPD sergeant at the 88th Precinct, just off the night shift.

Gloria serves pots of coffee, batches of scrambled eggs

and ham, piping-hot Italian bread I fetch from Gallo's Bakery. They argue, shout and curse, pore over the scratch sheet, calling each other imbeciles over every pick at Aqueduct that afternoon. To this day, these raucous mornings, when the world is full of hope and possibility, remain the best in my life.

This terrible evening they're "making a case," preparing to swear they were injured in the explosion. Similar things are happening on the many streets bordering the Red Hook piers. In the era before "containerization," dockworkers probably make up 50 percent of the working population of Gowanus. In a few days, they'll appear limping at the mobbed-up International Longshoremen's Association clinic on Court and Union Street or visit the sympathetic Italian American orthopedic surgeon, his calling card a Ferrari outside his brownstone office on Eighth Avenue. He'll write a report. They'll contact their lawyers and file a lawsuit.

In a place where, as soldiers say, no one has a "pot to piss in or a window to toss it out," everyone has a lawyer. Even me. Mine is Abraham Litke, whose office is on Court Street across from Borough Hall. I don't know if Abraham is a good lawyer, but he wears shiny suits and, one time, gives me his tie. When I'm hit by a taxi as I cross Flatbush Avenue—my knee twisted and lacerated, front teeth knocked out—he manages to lose. My parents had assured me my "case" would provide me college money.

Looking back at these men, all WWII combat veterans, not one of whom ever takes advantage of the GI Bill, most of whom die young from cigarettes and stress and brutal work, all of whom I love, I ask myself, "What level of desperation forces you to believe that crippling yourself for a few thousand dollars is the only option you have?"

CHAPTER TWELVE

Monduce

A weekly shave is the rare extravagance my father allows himself. This Saturday, I'm holding his callused hand as we cross Third Avenue and walk into Tony's Barbershop. A handful of men look up from newspapers, grunt, or nod hello, some in Italian. Joe lifts me—I'm five years old—into a miniature red fire truck by the front window, takes a seat against the mirrored wall with the others. I hesitate, then grab the steering wheel and begin sawing madly, racing the parade of cars and trucks passing outside the window.

"Vroom! Vroom!"

When I look around, a monster is limping toward me, leering, grimacing, making terrifying noises.

"Da!" I yell, trapped five feet off the ground. "Daaaa!"

Tony turns from his chair, looks at me. "Dat's-a Monduce," he says. "Is okay . . . Wants'a say 'allo."

"Daddy!"

I'm screaming, kicking the air as Joe pulls me out of the truck and through the door. I get a last look at the creature now standing in the doorway: small crooked metal rods running from thick high-top black shoes under his pants like a robot. Open mouth, rotting teeth.

He stays with me. Monduce and his drooling brother, Rafaele ("Rafe"), live across from Our Lady of Peace School at 504 Carroll Street, a brick building that in my mind is Dracula's castle and Frankenstein's laboratory. The two are everywhere: shining shoes in the barbershops and social clubs, at the newsstand on Fourth Avenue buying tiny De Nobili cigars ("Italian stinkers"), in doorways, behind cars. They communicate with shrieks and gestures and hold grudges. They're characters like the *ubriacos* (drunks) and *pazzi* (crazies) dotting the streets along the canal but disturbing on a much deeper level.

Under my desk during atomic bomb drills, I conjure up mutants with inhuman powers: Monduce and Rafe. Other kids swear they've seen Monduce run, appear like Dracula in different places at the same time, and throw the smooth green rock he keeps in his pocket like Mickey Mantle cutting down a runner at home plate. He carries a knife; I know he'll use it.

Superstition rules Gowanus. When my baby teeth fall out, my grandfather warns my mother not to put them in the trash lest a cat eat them, and I grow a mouthful of feline teeth. Clementina, my grandmother, dreads *il malocchio* more than germs. Gloria worries about polio (enema the prophylactic of choice). *Streghe* cast spells. We wear talismans—*corno* (horns), ribbons, crucifixes, saints, rosaries—around our necks and the steering columns of cars to keep evil at bay. There's a palm frond–draped altar on our bedroom dresser, the centerpiece a partially burned Yankee Doodle cupcake wrapper bearing the image of the Madonna.

I don't know *what* Monduce is. No one does. What science I absorb is medieval filtered through nuns ("God made them in His image and likeness"). Gossips pinch their thumbs and forefingers together, nod knowingly that Monduce and Rafe are the poisoned fruit of incest. There are others like them in the neighborhood.

Monduce takes a deep dislike to me. I don't taunt him like other kids; I study him like a bug in a jar. I pity him, and he senses it. He sees me staring into his apartment as he's coming out of the toilet. Catches me by his open cellar door. (I believe there's treasure hidden in the coal bin.) From then on, he stalks me, on stoops, the recreation center, the College restaurant on Fourth Avenue where he traps half a dozen of us eating late-night cheeseburgers. He corners me in the candy store among the Raisinets, jawbreakers, Sky Bars, Mary Janes, and pickled pigs' feet. I slip out of his grasp—he's as thin as a dandelion—long nails rasping against my shirt sleeve. Other nights, as I'm walking home with my father's newspapers, he's lurking in doorways.

He's already burst in on Johnny Bananas, the eighteen-year-old ball-breaker who lives upstairs from us. Johnny's asleep, and his mother, Rosie, AWOL from her knitting outside the house. (Under the reign of wiseguys, no one has to lock doors.) Monduce makes his way into Johnny's second-floor bedroom, leers into the teen's face—I imagine his foul breath—Johnny bursts awake and runs screaming down the stairs and into the street in his underwear.

At fifteen, I start my own business, a shoeshine operation. My equipment: a wooden ammunition box with hinged cover and rope handle, tins of black and brown polish, a bottle of wash, brush, and buffing cloths. An old Italian who runs a shoe repair shop gives me a cast-iron shoe rest, no charge. My brother Thomas models my father's dress shoes, Florsheim featherweights, so I can practice. The idea that I'm threatening a handicapped man's livelihood never crosses my mind.

Sunday morning, I'm in front of the building catty-corner from the barbershop hoping to catch men coming out of church with their wives. They walk right by me, minds on afternoon baseball, and the simmering tomato sauce wafting out of every house. Jimmy "Blubberhead" Barbella, my godfather, walks up Carroll, coffee mug in one hand, cigarette in the other. Half asleep, heading for the Glory Social Club, where the all-day card games are already going.

"*Ue cumpariell!*" he says using the diminutive (sounds like "way goombardeel"). "Where's your father?"

Best friends before the war. I have a picture of them wearing zoot suits.

"He's home. Cooking, of course."

"Don't be a wise guy! He's a good man!"

"Shine?" I ask.

The last thing he wants, but says, "Yeah, go 'head."

In a flash, I'm squatting, cleaner, polish, brushes, and flannel buffing cloth at the ready. Real shoeshine guys make the cloths snap like firecrackers. I can't, so I try to keep polish off his socks, black, beautiful, silk, transparent.

"Whatta you doing this stuff for?" he asks, flicking his cigarette toward the curb.

I charge fifteen cents a shine, maybe a quarter with tip. I can scrounge up empty soda bottles from the mountains of trash dumped in the lots by the canal and make more money. Grocers pay a five-cent deposit for each bottle returned. I'm trying to convince myself manual labor is a career calling. I'm also afraid of the unknown, of being alone, of losing friends and family should I venture out of Gowanus, a fear hard to shake.

"I don't know," I say, unable to find the words.

He hands me a dollar.

When I look up, Muzzi, another of my father's friends, is waiting. I grin, nod, and get to work on his loafers. I keep my head down as I clean, polish, and buff the soft leather. Out of nowhere, a thick black boot flashes in front of my nose, kicks at my shine box.

"What the fuck!" Muzzi shouts.

Shrieking, Monduce is clumsily stomping my tins and bottles. I'm paralyzed, squatting on the sidewalk. Muzzi steps down, grabs him by the throat, hesitates, and releases him.

"What the fuck!" he shouts in Monduce's face.

I scramble to my feet. Funzi and Vincent Manzo from the Glory Social Club are walking toward us. Monduce is crawling on the sidewalk grabbing at Muzzi's pant leg. Funzi lifts him to his feet. He's still howling, gesticulating at me.

"This is his corner!" Vincent Manzo says. He stoops, picks up my shoeshine stuff, dumps it in the apartment building's garbage can. He turns, reaches into his pocket, hands me twenty dollars.

"Leave him the fuck alone!"

He's talking to me.

I'm out of business.

✦ ✦ ✦

In the sixties, blue laws restrict Sunday sales. John's Candy Store must close at one p.m., when my parents are about to serve the meal they've spent hours preparing. Sunday is also the one time Joe allows soft drinks—Coca-Cola and Hoffman—in the house. Cash in hand, I jog up Carroll Street, cross Third Avenue, already tasting the ice-cold soda John keeps in his old-fashioned icebox.

Monduce lives next door. Hurrying home, I never look back. Twenty minutes later, I'm sitting down to a first course of ravioli, meatballs, and braciole when someone pounds the front door.

"I'll get it."

I'm out of my chair, thinking it's Dennis Pots, who shows up at all hours. I walk through the parlor, pull open the first plywood door with its ribbon of bells, then the heavier front door, never glancing through its triangular window. Howling, Monduce lunges or lurches at, or maybe falls on, me, scratching at my face. Gasping, I stumble backward, hit the floor, catch the dead look in his eyes.

I push him off, get to my feet—my three brothers are screaming—sprint through the parlor, the dining room where Joe and Gloria sit speechless, the kitchen, into the yard, and under the persimmon tree and jump over the low cinder-block fence into the Catapano yard. They're having dinner. Everyone is. I'm running through the streets, imagining a goblin on my tail.

Half an hour later, I've circled the block and stand peering through the door glass. Crawling on the dining room floor, Monduce is kissing my mother's foot.

His way of swearing he's telling the truth.

✦ ✦ ✦

By the seventies, Monduce's world is in upheaval. The Italian immigrants who sheltered and protected him are passing away. Rafe shuttles back and forth to Lechworth Village in Rockland County, a primitive assisted living facility where he'll die. I'm in college writing pompous sociology papers on them ("Monduce: A Neighborhood Phenomenon"). My surviving friends are outgrowing our childhood. Church *and* wiseguys are shedding influence. White flight is emptying ethnic Brooklyn. Yuppies are gathering on the horizon. Crime, violence, and addiction are our new demons. No longer feared, Monduce is abused, mocked, and slapped around by punks blind to the shadows spreading over their own lives. I witness it all.

My own fears transform to shame.

CHAPTER THIRTEEN

An Immigrant's Tale

Ernie Palmieri sat by the radiators in Sister Mary Malachy's classroom. I sat a few rows away in the dead zone in the back of the crowded room reserved for misfits and troublemakers, tracing carvings left behind by generations of parochial school penitents.

Tall with startling green eyes and coal-black hair, Palmieri was no wiseguy. Even in elementary school, he was marking time, a middle child with seven siblings. His parents, Rocco, a shoemaker, and Maria, a seamstress, emigrated from Calabria when Ernie was six. His twin sisters, Elvira and Delia, were blessed with that olive complexion you see in medieval frescoes, together one of those immigrant families who blossomed even in Gowanus.

Ernie lived on Fifth Avenue where trees lined the slope leading to Prospect Park. He mostly avoided Malachy's wrath, waltzed stiffly with the rest of us in our overblown Christmas production of Verdi's aria "La donna è mobile" in the parish recreation center. My cousin JuJu and his thugs jeered and hooted.

And then Ernie was gone.

We were just fourteen years old.

I went to an all-boys Catholic high school in Park Slope, wore ill-fitting jackets and ties, stiff white shirts the Chinese laundry starched for twenty cents. Endured more years of beating and bullying, this time by Christian Brothers. I learned things.

Ernie went to Manual Training (now John Jay High School) on Seventh Avenue, dropped out, and went to work. Walking home from St. Augustine, I'd spot him behind the counter at Ben's Pork Store near his house, a place fragrant with wheels of Parmigiano, provolone, and prosciutto di Parma hanging from the ceiling, marinated mushrooms, roasted peppers, and wheels of *cervellata*—smells and tastes that intoxicate me to this day. I pop in, maybe twenty-five cents in my pocket; Ernie, in his white butcher's apron, winks and sneaks me a hunk of *soppressata.*

In 1965, I'm a freshman at Brooklyn College. Ernie and his older brother, Julio, are already planning to open a butcher shop near Bay Ridge. I have no idea who I am or what I want to do with my life. I am achingly lonely as the umbilical that binds me to Gowanus begins to rupture. War is on the horizon.

We're eighteen years old.

Ernie meets a girl, Mary Lou Lobianco, he wants to marry. She dumps him. When the call-ups begin in earnest in 1965, I, native-born, can't think of enough ways to avoid Vietnam. Ernie Palmieri, an immigrant, follows Julio and enlists. After basic training, Ernie is assigned to the army's 71st Assault Helicopter Company, jockeying thin-skinned UH-1 Huey choppers into very bad places, inserting and extracting grunts, pulling out the wounded and dead.

I don't know any of this. Most people I know wouldn't care. I'm teaching English to mechanics at Automotive High in Williamsburg, a very different Williamsburg from today's. I find my father's records in the school basement. He made it past second year, then left to fight in the Pacific.

On Carroll Street, we listen to doo-wop music, the Four Seasons, Young Rascals, Sinatra, like the wiseguys in the Capri Club. I'm late coming to the Beatles and Stones, but I remember, of all things, "Galveston," a country song about the war, not mocking or bitter but devastating in its power to pierce me like a dagger and capture the longing and loss of war.

I still hear your sea waves crashin' . . .
I clean my gun and dream of Galveston.

There's a line about a girl, a memory of running on a beach, wondering if she'll be there when he gets home. I'd never run on a beach with a girl, but there was another song seemingly about a telephone lineman in Kansas. I understood that guy better than I knew myself.

I become a reporter. The war ends, but another is beginning: Vietnam veterans are being ignored or debased as druggies and losers. Out of concern, guilt, or a need to make amends, the working-class kid who missed the working-class war, I begin covering Vietnam veterans. I write the first story on women vets—skilled nurses, kids themselves—who tended the horribly wounded and comforted the dying, for *Newsweek.* One of these women, Lola McGourty, is still my friend forty-five years later. I write a book, *Uneasy Warriors,* about Vietnam's Green Berets, JFK's own soldiers, elevated as heroes and cast down in defeat. I go to Hanoi to report on Chuck Searcy, an American vet who returned to assist children damaged by Agent Orange and the aftereffects of the conflict. I'm there a month and find a new generation of Vietnamese, very different from the waves of battle-hardened, determined soldiers who gave the Americans all they could handle. The posters in Hanoi now depict B-52s dropping long strings of Coca-Cola. The "American War" is a distant memory. Young Vietnamese want cell phones and flat-screen TVs. I see obese children.

In Washington, DC, I find Ernie Palmieri at the Vietnam Veterans Memorial. He's waiting there for me (panel 13E, line 23). Ernie was killed on December 8, 1966, the Feast of the Immaculate Conception, on a mission extracting soldiers who'd come under attack near Củ Chi, the site of a massive underground tunnel complex built by the Vietcong that is now a major tourist destination. After-action reports suggest the bullet may have been fired by a sniper in a schoolhouse the choppers spared because kids were playing outside the building.

Ernie's parents, Rocco and Maria, were waiting at Penn Station to claim his body when it arrived from Dover Air Force Base. If they were anything like my parents, a trip in the middle of the night to the City would be daunting. Specialist 4th Class Ernest Palmieri, the serious kid who sat by the whistling radiators in Our Lady of Peace School, who made his First Communion in a white suit with me, who attended Mass every Sunday—attendance was mandatory—was buried in Long Island National Cemetery.

The story doesn't end there. On August 16, 2008, US Army UH-1 helicopter (tail number 65-10068), Ernie's chopper, arrived in tiny Mineral Wells, Texas, where it was mounted on a steel pillar as one of the city's National Vietnam War Museum exhibits. Four men from Ernie's unit, the 71st Assault Helicopter Company, old men themselves, showed up to honor him. The museum offered free hot dogs to the first five hundred attendees.

Even this was nearly a decade in the past. And yet, in 2017, when the media mentioned the death of Glen Campbell and inevitably began playing the haunting strains of "Galveston," Ernie came alive again, as I knew him so long ago, and the loss was such I thought my heart would burst.

CHAPTER FOURTEEN

Aliens Among Us

People here are not used to any kind of "different" coming into the neighborhood.

—Patrick Emer, Butler Street

Their appearance is so startling they might have landed in a flying saucer. In saffron robes, men with shaved heads and *shikha* (topknots) and women marking percussive beats with *manjeera* (finger cymbals) march single file along Henry Street stopping housewives heading to Cammareri's Bakery and Tuddy Balsamo's fish store in their tracks. Black-clad *nonnas* cross themselves. Old men outside the Citizens of Pozzallo social club put down espressos and *Il Progresso* and gape.

Over and over, the strangers chant sixteen unintelligible words.

Hare Krishna, Hare Krishna, Krishna Krishna, Hare, Hare,
Hare Rama, Hare Rama, Rama, Rama, Hare, Hare.

By the time they reach 439 Henry Street, formerly home to a beloved order of nuns ministering to the poor and sick for half a century, they've drawn a pack of giggling urchins who dance alongside them, shouting:

Harry Kirschner! Harry Kirschner!

"Da fuck is this?" From the stoops along Henry, teens hoot. A few flip cigarettes at the procession.

Unfazed, the marchers, members of the International Society for Krishna Consciousness, disappear through the redbrick mansion's double doors, unaware that they've crossed an invisible but very real border dividing Gowanus from the outside world. (Ironically, Winston Churchill's mother, Jeanette Jerome, was born a few doors away.) Next morning, they troop out, chanting, beating drums, clanging cymbals, startling mothers escorting children to PS 29 on Kane Street. Begging bowls extended, they walk ten blocks to the Bergen Street subway station, where Anthony Leone sits reading a schoolbook. "This guy comes up, places a magazine on the page I'm reading," Leone remembered. "I politely tell him 'I have my own reading.'

"'This is better news!'

"I tell him if I don't read mine, it'll be bad news for me. What I want to say is 'Get the fuck away from me! Or it'll be bad news for you!'"

They board the train and head for Washington Square Park, Times Square, Central Park, Broadway, Columbia University, where they beg, proselytize, hawk incense and tracts, drone the mantra invoking Lord Krishna's compassion, protection, and love. Evening, robes dragging, they return to a scant vegetarian meal and sleep on mattresses scattered on the floors. In an era of free love, sex is prohibited, except for procreation, and then rarely.

◆ ◆ ◆

I spot them outside the Anthony Anastasio Memorial Wing of the longshoremen's medical center on Union Street, or sometimes by Cammareri's Bakery, where Nicolas Cage will seduce Cher in *Moonstruck.* Very little from outside the neighborhood penetrates, so I stand gawking, chewing a hunk of bread still warm from the oven as dozens reeking of musk and sandalwood, sporting those crazy haircuts, flood the neighborhood like a circus parade. To me, they're mysterious, otherworldly, but in the closed, incurious world of Gowanus, they are seen as aliens and worse.

They commit an unforgiveable sin. As neighbors stare in disbelief, they haul a statue of the Virgin Mary left by the nuns into the backyard, dismember it, and toss the pieces in the trash. This in a place where on Good Friday, bands thump funeral dirges and sobbing men march behind Our Lady of Sorrows—her heart pierced by swords—and a glass casket containing the crucified Christ. A place where people hesitate to throw away dried-out fronds after Palm Sunday, regard broken rosaries and cracked plaster saints as holy objects. My mother keeps a partially burned wrapper of a Yankee Doodle cupcakes package because she sees the Virgin Mary's image seared onto it. I see it too.

The desecration triggers a tsunami of anger that never dissipates. Cobble Hill and Carroll Gardens, bustling neighborhoods that back up to the piers, are also very much working-class Italian enclaves, inward-looking, wary, protective of their own. Families are intact, multigenerational, outsiders unwelcome. Men are dockworkers, women housewives, all bound by blood, marriage, and the Catholic Church. Old-timers make red wine in the cellars, play raucous bocce games in Carroll Park. Bakeries, butchers, pastry stores, and latticini line the streets, bookies and wiseguys embedded like almonds in torrone. Joe Gallo and his gang lurk on President Street, attuned to the slightest vibration in their web.

And now, as if the Gowanus were the Ganges, an explosion of otherworldly followers of Bhaktivedanta, a penniless guru arrived from India on a freighter. In a neighborhood where immigrant and first-generation laborers struggle to pay rent and put food on the table, he proclaims the material world and its riches meaningless. Martyrs and suffering—parts of a bedrock Catholic (and wiseguy) doctrine—do not illumine the road to heaven, the guru teaches. Joy, peace, and happiness flow from *abject* devotion to Lord Krishna, a flute-playing deity with indigo skin, a peacock feather in his hair, and many wives.

In 1965, Bhaktivedanta began his outreach among the hippies, drunks, druggies, and dreamers of the East Village. At Tompkins Square Park, chanting the Krishna mantra, he found an audience disenchanted with materialism and aching for life on a higher plane. By 1971, George Harrison and Timothy Leary are Krishna converts, as are the legions of chanting beggars at American airports and a generation as disaffected as the Beats of the 1950s.

In '72, fifty-odd men, women, infants, and children arrive at 439 Henry Street. Their worship, accompanied by incense, bells, oil lamps, and flowers, singing, and the endless chanting that will soon drive locals mad is not so different from what I encounter at Our Lady of Peace Parish. They paint the convent chapel yellow, fuchsia, purple, orange, and cerise, build a throne for Swami Bhaktivedanta. This first temple is only a mile from the Gowanus Canal.

Not an enlightened choice.

Outsiders are never welcome in Gowanus. They're certainly not "friends we haven't yet met." A long-haired jazz musician with guitar and girlfriend arouses the ire of the "*maldicenti*" when he moves to 456 Carroll Street. Three floors up, Rosita, a longtime resident who poses nude in her window, gets a pass. In the late sixties, a dozen Gypsies, including an aged "king," arrive in a caravan of rattletrap cars, park in spaces reserved for Mikey Romanelli and the Goose, crowd into Dr. D'Amato's old ground-floor office on the same corner where *guaglione* ("wallyos") shout and gamblers handicap action, stroll into Rosina's grocery for sandwiches, Twinkies, and cigarettes, and allow toddlers to wander streets thick with traffic, outraging my mother and aunts.

The king (he drives a Cadillac) helps me tune my ratty Triumph TR4. I befriend three younger Gypsies, body-and-fender men who tell me fantastic lies about their Long Island adventures. They insist they used a can of spray paint and a pound of liverwurst—it was Sunday; the auto supply shops were closed, but the Jewish deli open—to repair a car in Lynbrook. "It worked great until a dog came sniffing." They say they came back and seduced the suburbanite's wife and her neighbor.

A mad new world has been delivered to my door.

Then neighborhood punks harass, threaten, slap the young guys around. They smash the king's windshield. It continues for months—Gypsies, immovable; me, cowardly and ashamed—until the old king passes away. Days later, they're gone.

It happens again when an "undesirable" (i.e., Black) family moves into an apartment next to my aunt's candy store, only much more quickly. But when in a rage my uncle Punchy, jealous of his wife and the odd factory worker who comes in for cigarettes, shoves his own jukebox into the gutter (forty-five-rpm records roll merrily toward the canal), no one utters a word. He's lived on Carroll Street his whole life.

Puerto Ricans move into an apartment building on Carroll above Fifth Avenue. Italian "South Brooklyn Boys" battle Puerto Rican "Bishops" just like *West Side Story*, only the Bishops have been radicalized by Armando Sandoval, a chubby Marxist I know from Brooklyn College. A turf war, a gang war, is now a war of liberation, which makes wiseguys in the Nestor Club—my erstwhile heroes—oppressors. A bomb detonates in the apartment building. The Puerto Ricans disappear. Armando, shot in the ass, survives to cut sugarcane in Castro's Cuba.

In Cobble Hill, merciless wiseguys shut down a Hasidic school and a Muslim academy. Meanwhile, the Krishnas keep pushing their packets of incense, hassling strangers—sometimes the wrong strangers. On Court Street, a guy sets a packet of incense aflame, then flips it back into a Krishna's face. On Sackett, a group of Krishnas march into Court Sash, a neighborhood lumberyard, to pressure the owner for a donation. Patrick Emer, one of the neighborhood urchins, remembers, "He [the owner] had a two-by-four in his hand, and it didn't look like he was gonna donate it."

The Krishnas host open houses and weddings—humble fare—attended by ill-at-ease parents, siblings, a few curious locals. In August '71, George Harrison, headlining the Concert for Bangladesh at Madison Square Garden, shows up on Henry Street. "Me and my friends ran over there," remembered Phil Florentino. "It was jammed with kids from the nabe. George was wearing jeans and a brown vest!" Florentino returns to the temple, figuring "'George was here, they must be cool.' When they lit the incense, I choked and ran out. I only smelled this stuff in church."

An unspoken Pax Romana protects young women and yuppie families moving into Carroll Gardens and Boerum Hill. (They're viewed as harmless, oddball "hippies" until they drive up housing prices astronomically.) No peace for the Krishnas who are literal pacifists. Tensions between cult and community escalate over the next years, until windows are being smashed, fireworks tossed, thugs lie in wait for Krishnas to emerge from the subway. "I know people who slapped a few when they walked down Kane Street," remembers Emer with a laugh.

Some of the Krishnas are teenagers, lost, lonely, confused, and hungry. Connie Sanfrantello and her mother, Antoinette (renowned in the neighborhood for her handmade jelly apples), run a fruit store at 418 Henry Street, across from the temple. They feed and shelter the runaways who show up at their door. It's the reverse for a nine-year-old urchin named Josephine Sulsenti. She runs up and down the temple's front steps ringing the doorbell constantly to "torment them." Eventually invited in—the Krishnas are gentle—she removes her shoes and joins the chanting. "It's like a game." Then her mother, a single parent, stops in to play cards. All's fine until the Krishnas mention they want to adopt Josephine and move her to "somewhere in the Midwest" (most likely a new temple in West Virginia). Her mother freaks out, ordering her, "*Never* go there anymore."

Fireworks give way to firebombs. In December '73, Democratic boss James Mangano arrives from his Union Street headquarters to deal with what the newspapers describe as "a very ticklish situation." The neighborhood wants the Krishnas gone. Period. Mangano warns the absentee landlord who's holding a seven-year lease, "This can't go on." When the landlord balks, Mangano, whose own father was shot in a Gowanus dispute, shrugs. "People may burn your place down."

Years later, when word circulates that I'm revisiting the Krishnas' sojourn in what's become a very upscale Cobble Hill, an IM arrives on my computer.

> Vincent:
>
> The Orthodox Jewish school was burned down by my uncle and a few other wise guys [*sic*] in the neighborhood to get them out . . . The Krishnas moved in not long after the school was torched . . . They had no furniture or clothes or anything. They wore sheets and all they had inside were blankets and pillows . . . A few guys from the neighborhood went and had a talk with them.

An offer even a swami couldn't refuse.

CHAPTER FIFTEEN

Jimmy Psycho

I didn't have much.

So I was furious when Gloria gave my favorite shirt to Jimmy Psycho, an iridescent silver-and-green guayabera that sparkled in the sun. She just reached into the hall closet right in front of me and handed it to him.

My mother was like that her whole life. When she died, folks from the St. Vincent de Paul Society, the Holy Name Society, this confraternity, that sodality kept showing up at our door for months, seeking the few dollars she'd committed to their charities. She'd serve them coffee and Drake's pound cake I'd buy at Farmer Jones's grocery.

She didn't have much.

Jimmy was my first cousin, Gloria's handicapped sister Jenny's son, one of half a dozen siblings who terrorized and charmed Gowanus for thirty years, their nicknames still etched on walls and in memories—Alibi Ike, Jimmy Psycho, JuJu, Popeye Anthony, Richie Mel. A sister, Carol the Bug, was as troublesome as the boys.

They lived above Mariuchelle's grocery on Third Avenue, a bedlam of shouts and screams and laughter that made our house seem staid. In the 1950s, the patriarch, my uncle Fat, stood jeering on a picket line during a dockworkers' strike when a tractor trailer driven by an amped-up Southerner ran him down. No word on the driver, but for years Uncle Fat limped into neighborhood groceries and butcher shops, took whatever he wanted, glared at the frightened merchants, and told them, "Bill the fucking wiseguys!"

Jimmy shows up unkempt, sallow, shivering in a dirty T-shirt, strung out. Gloria tries to feed him, but he can't handle anything but sweets and chocolate Yoo-hoo. She pulls a few dollars from her purse, grabs my shirt from the closet, and helps him button it. Like biblical Joseph, I'm stripped of my coat of many colors.

Jimmy is a taller, better-looking, charismatic version of me. Everyone knows everyone else in Gowanus, so the fact that I'm Jimmy Psycho's cousin shields me from the worst punks. He's the leader of the South Brooklyn Boys LAMF ("like a motherfucker") in the never-ending wars against the Untouchable Bishops (Puerto Rican) and the Apaches (Black and Puerto Rican) street gangs. These are bloody battles, fought with knives, chains, and zip guns over a few blocks of cracked sidewalk and the overgrown lots on both sides of the canal.

When junk (heroin) makes another of its cyclical passes across Gowanus, South Brooklyn Boys, Bishops, and Apaches fall like dominos, JuJu and Jimmy both. I remember Jimmy and Robert Schiano running along Nevins Street, pushing a rack of men's suits they'd somehow stolen from Abraham & Straus on Fulton Street. In Gowanus, these deliveries were today's Amazon. My first camera, a Konica SLR, was delivered right to my door, as was an IBM Selectric I practiced on after I was admitted to Columbia University's journalism school.

Jimmy is so strung-out he decapitates scores of parking meters for the dimes inside, leaves the bases standing like a pine forest after a hurricane. One day, Uncle Fat corners the dealer who first sold Jimmy heroin on Union and Fifth Avenue. He bites the guy's ear off, though later he goes into the parking meter business with Jimmy.

At a Labor Day barbecue in my grandmother's backyard, my cousins Jimmy and Johnny Pomarico, brawny NYPD officers, leap the fence when they spot Jimmy and his kid brother, JuJu, breaking into telephone company vans on Nevins Street. They pummel them until the boys plead to be taken to the station house. A few years later, Jimmy's girlfriend, a blond Norwegian nurse from Bay Ridge, tries to break his habit. Next, I hear she's an addict and Jimmy's her pimp.

I hate him.

In 1968, I ride the grimy IRT Flatbush Avenue Line to Brooklyn College, sit in droning chemistry lectures with hundreds of students. I've won a Regents Scholarship, but I can't afford not to work. My Gowanus job experience—manual labor, eyes-shut gigs for wiseguys—has not prepared me for the larger world. So I drive a laundry truck in and out of Manhattan for Herbert Pearl, a choleric man with a bad heart. Dry-cleaning is free, but not pressing. I work in a firetrap Williamsburg gasket factory for a fellow Brooklyn College grad named David Ross. My paychecks bounce, and he runs back and forth dodging Italian loan sharks who eventually storm the factory.

Gloria tells me Jimmy is at Daytop Village, an experimental drug rehabilitation center somewhere on Staten

Island and is doing well. Determined to leave that world behind, I avoid thinking about him or his siblings. One night in the college library, I'm thumbing through *Newsweek* when a rave review of an off-Broadway play, *The Concept,* jumps out at me. It's produced and performed by Daytop's recovering addicts. The critic Jack Kroll singles out one searing performance. Of course it's Jimmy's.

He was always charismatic. When he's invited to the White House for a command performance, I'm sorting dirty restaurant linen in the back of a panel truck in Bedford–Stuyvesant. Years later, when I wind up working at *Newsweek,* I walk past Kroll's office—books piled floor to ceiling like stalagmites—every day. I want to tell him how much his review mattered to Jimmy . . . and me, how life-changing it was—but that wouldn't be true.

Jimmy stays at Daytop as a counselor. Given his history and fragile ego, five minutes of fame is intoxicating. When he leaves Staten Island, he tells me he *needs* to prove himself in the real world. But he's just a chain-smoking, twitchy thirty-year-old dropout with a history of drug abuse, zero life skills, and a criminal record. The yellowing newspaper clippings in his wallet and his trip to the White House are met with shrugs. He refuses to return to Daytop.

Years pass. The next time I see Jimmy, he's covered in soot, reeking of alcohol, beaten down. He's a chimney sweep, cleaning furnaces in Prospect Heights apartment buildings. I have no idea what to say or do. He asks about "Aunt Gloria." I stuff twenty dollars in his uniform pocket and hurry away.

✦ ✦ ✦

December 1990. Lights twinkle in the shop windows on Seventh Avenue; men hawk Christmas trees as carols play over tinny speakers. It's freezing cold. Gloria's throat cancer has returned. She's been in Methodist Hospital's cancer ward since Thanksgiving. At Christmas, the tired decorations and false cheer in the hospital are a mockery. My brothers, cousins, aunts, and uncles visit my mother in shifts. This evening, I'm reading, when I hear tumult by the elevators. I get up, walk into the corridor. Nurses, orderlies, interns, and security men in a scrum around a skinny disheveled guy. His shout breaks my heart. "Aunt Gloria! Aunt Gloria!"

It's Jimmy.

"He's family! Let him alone!"

The security guards look at me oddly, shrug, and walk away.

"Where's Aunt Gloria?"

He's not wearing a coat. It's fifteen degrees.

"Jimmy, it's Cousin Vinny."

"I know who you are," he mumbles.

In her room, images of Jesus, Mary, St. Francis of Assisi, and my children are taped to the walls. Uneaten meals in plastic containers line the windowsills.

"I'm here to see Aunt Gloria."

I choke up. "I know why you're here."

Jimmy is thin, pale, shivering, wearing wrinkled black slacks and a grimy white shirt—his best clothes.

"How's she doing?" he says hoarsely.

"Not good."

He's silent a long moment. "My sister told me, so I came."

"How you doing?"

"Not so good," he says, looking at the floor.

"How did you get here?"

"Walked."

"What?"

I grab my coat from the foot of the bed, wrap it around his shoulders.

"Take it. I've got a car . . . Please, Jimmy."

Gloria stirs. Instantly, he's at her bedside.

"Aunt Gloria, it's me," he says, taking her hand. "Jimmy."

Maybe she squeezed; maybe she didn't. I like to think she did. Gloria smiles wanly and drops back on her pillow.

"I gotta buy her something."

Gloria hasn't eaten in weeks. She's being fed liquid nutrients through a tube in her stomach that keeps pulling loose.

"Jimmy . . ."

"Please, Vinny, I got money," he says, reaching into his pocket.

He didn't have much.

We ride the elevator, walk among the visitors in the ground-floor gift shop. Jimmy stares carefully at the gum and magazines, the cheap jewelry, the rosaries; finally, he picks out a small bouquet and two lemon ice pops. He hands them to me and heads out the door.

I never see him alive again.

CHAPTER SIXTEEN

I'm Arrested for Murder

I'm running along Fifth Avenue, giggling hysterically, a pint of Tango detonating in my skull, Joe Bo and Richie sprinting beside me. At St. John's Place, I toss the car antenna in my hand under a parked van and keep running.

I'm fifteen years old, but the clerk in the Fourth Avenue liquor store never blinks when I pull the few greasy bills from my Wranglers. What am I thinking on the rare school night my father allows me out? Girls, but that's not going to happen, so vengeance.

For two years, in jacket and tie, I've been forced to stand in a long line of goofballs in the middle of the street on Park Place while Brother Jerome conducts a mandated fire drill or marches us—St. Jean-Baptiste de La Salle's finest—to Mass. On the stoops, grinning, pimply thugs—the Untouchable Bishops—and their sexy *chicas,* Puerto Rican flags embroidered on their jean jackets, jeer.

"*¡Cabrónes!*" (Assholes!)

"*¡Mamabichos!*" (Dicksuckers!)

"*¡Pendejos!*" (Idiots!)

I blush.

Richie's a sensitive guy, an aspiring doo-wop singer, and Joe Bo's nickname is "Dilly-Dally," so this behind-the-lines commando raid must have been my idea, likely another fantasy come to unfortunate life. A few twists of a radio antenna on a parked car and I'm a dashing swordsman, but as we cross Union and head toward Flatbush Avenue, the burden of command is weighing on me. Or maybe the rotgut vodka and Tango gurgling in my stomach. Stealthily, we advance past Joe Cuomo's darkened luncheonette, turn onto Sterling Place, where we startle a policeman, a big guy, his face the pink of corned beef, talking on a call box phone.

He turns, stares at us.

We stare back.

A long moment passes.

"Stop!" he yells, dropping the phone.

"STOP!"

Of course, we run, heading for Union Street, the border between Italian and Puerto Rican South Brooklyn, overcome by the hilarity of intoxication and the fat cop we've left agape. By Degraw, I'm winded, fighting not to throw up, and then I glance back—the officer, huffing and puffing, peaked hat askew, is half a block behind us.

And closing.

"Ahhh!"

I start running, this time at panic speed, around the corner on Fifth Avenue, onto Union, past the Democratic Club—I've just applied for a patronage job at the post office; now I'm an outlaw—not stopping until I'm halfway to Fourth Avenue. Joe Bo, no fool, darts between parked cars, crosses Union, making for the safe harbor that is Gowanus. I stand holding my side—Richie gasping beside me—drunk, confused, trying to figure out what the fuck is happening. A cop chasing us for blocks over a stupid antenna?

Fear, real fear, drips like acid in my gut as a blue Pontiac coupe jumps the curb onto the sidewalk, cutting off any chance of escape.

"The fuck!"

The same cop pops out of the passenger door like a clown fired out of a circus cannon, hand on his pistol.

"Don't even fuckin' move!"

I'm hoping to go to college, my uncle Sonny is an NYPD sergeant in the 88th Precinct a few miles away, my outsize cousin Johnny is a Tactical Patrol Force lieutenant, and my father is a lunatic. Getting a JD (juvenile delinquent) card, an official record of a criminal charge brought against a minor, is unthinkable.

Pouring sweat, the cop bulls us against a wrought-iron fence outside an apartment building, pats us down, and slaps me hard in the face.

I say nothing. Richie moans.

"Get moving!"

"Where?" Richie squeaks. "My mother's gonna kill me."

His mother, big as a man, keeps her three sons, Richie, Paulie, and Spongehead, mostly locked in their apartment, their luxuriant sexual fantasies rampant and well known in Gowanus. Richie's brothers are nicknamed "Laurel and Hard-on."

"SHUT THE FUCK UP!"

Pow! The cop slaps him.

He marches us to the Pontiac, releases the seat, shoves Richie, then me—banging our heads—in the back, then squeezes into the front bucket seat, arm out the window. People stand gawking, strangers, but I'm a car nut and I know this car, a '63 Grand Prix, red interior, 389-cubic-inch V8. I've seen it on Degraw Street. A neighborhood guy.

"Bergen Street!" the cop—let's call him Murphy—orders the driver, a good-looking older guy, maybe twenty-five. I see the driver stiffen. Some Irish cops label neighborhood Italians "white niggers." The rest probably question the term "white."

"Let's go!" The amped-up cop slaps the side of the door, a cowboy spurring a horse.

In Gowanus, Bergen Street is the 78th Precinct station house, a grim five-story limestone box, a bank whose currency is fear and pain. These are the cops I see strolling into the Capri Club on Saturday afternoons and emerging with brown paper bags stuffed with cash "for the captain," who "coop" for hours in the lot behind the John P. Carlson paint factory drinking whiskey and accepting blow jobs from junkie prostitutes. From behind mountains of trash, Ernie and I occasionally mortar them with beer bottles and rocks.

The driver backs into the street, makes a U-turn, then a left on Fifth Avenue. He stares at me in the rearview mirror.

"Officer," he says carefully when he stops for the light at Flatbush, "I know these kids. They good kids. Is there a way we can handle this . . . problem . . . out here?"

"Good kids?" the cop barks. "Punks killed a spic on Garfield Place, then ran right into me. Weren't they surprised!"

A bolt of heat shoots through me.

"I'm nailing them for murder."

My heart is pounding so hard, I can't speak.

The driver crosses Flatbush in silence.

I'm scared shitless. Richie's sobbing.

We pull up to 65 Sixth Avenue. The burly cop gets out; two uniformed patrolmen hurry down the precinct steps. They pull us out of the back seat; the Grand Prix slips away and disappears. Inside, we're marched past the desk officer, no paperwork, no phone call, no questions, no booking, nothing.

Word of Murphy's collar spreads.

"Nice work!" a cop congratulates the beaming Murphy. No one wears an ID badge. We're walked into a large room painted puke green with a grimy tile floor, scattered chairs and tables, a calendar, half-empty Styrofoam coffee cups, a duty roster on the wall. Cops move in and out. I've seen this room before. In a much-circulated news photo in Gowanus, a teenaged Carmine Persico, later head of the Colombo family, and six members of the Garfield Boys street gang are lined up along a wall after being brought in when a teen was murdered in a gang war in Prospect Park. I'm staring at that wall when Murphy pushes me into a chair, stands behind me. Another cop does the same with Richie.

I'm trembling but rapidly sobering up. My Catholic schoolboy side tells me this is a mistake and will soon be cleared up, maybe even before my father discovers I'm not asleep in my room. Then the neighborhood code of honor kicks in: "protect" the liquor store owner and don't "rat out" Joe Bo, leaving me nothing to say.

Murphy demands, "Who's the other punk?" I don't answer. He slaps me in the back of the head.

"THE FUCK IS THE OTHER GUY?"

I can't answer.

Now I'm the wiseguy. Over the next hours, I'm slapped, punched, pulled out of my chair and slammed against the wall, barraged with screams and curses—Murphy's attempt to elicit a confession. Same with Richie on the other side of the room. Different uniformed patrolmen take turns with us. I never see a detective.

I do learn my "crime." Earlier in the evening, two "greaseballs" show up at a Puerto Rican quinceañera, one with a shotgun, walk up the stoop, ring the doorbell, and the *'mano* who answers takes a blast of twelve-gauge pellets to the chest.

Years later, when I'm in college, my cousin Johnny, the TPF lieutenant, patiently explains why it's necessary to stuff the occasional recalcitrant "Negro" suspect into a metal locker and slam the locker with nightsticks: "These are really bad guys, Vinny, and we know they're guilty." He also tells me "coloreds" have had their penises and testicles splayed on a tabletop and beaten (that, I choose not to believe). He's honestly disappointed when I don't empathize.

Murphy, a lowly beat cop, is convinced he's nailed the killers, and he's not letting go. Promotion, merit-based raises, a detective's shield, bragging rights at Farrell's and the Shamrock Tavern on Flatbush Avenue, maybe a plate of the gigantic pork chops and vinegar peppers cops favor at Two Toms restaurant. He orders Richie to get up and they disappear. Time passes. Murphy returns alone. Smiling. He says Richie confessed and named me the triggerman.

I'm fifteen years old. I see my life collapsing before me. I still say nothing.

✦ ✦ ✦

Sometime after midnight, two detectives and a gaggle of uniformed officers frog-march half a dozen surly teens into the squad room. I recognize some of them: Joe Silver and his Golden Guineas, a violent street gang whose turf includes Fifth Avenue and Garfield Place. One of them the killer.

Murphy stands gaping.

I don't dare look at him.

At some point, he orders me to stand up. Without a word, he walks me to the precinct entrance, arm around my shoulder like we're old buddies. At the top of the concrete steps, he punches me full force in the stomach and kicks me down the three steps. I get up and start running and never stop until I'm home.

Weeks pass. When I have the courage, I ask my uncle Sonny, the NYPD sergeant, to stop by the 78th Precinct. He tells me there is no record of my ever having been there that night. Am I sure I have the right precinct?

Fast forward to 1968. My classmates at Brooklyn College, mostly middle-class Jewish kids from Midwood, Sheepshead Bay, and Flatbush, have this wholesome view of the smiling police officer who directs traffic and helps old ladies cross the street. One afternoon, when I spot dozens of grim NYPD officers surrounding the campus during a Vietnam War protest, I disappear. Sure enough, they come charging in and beat the shit out of anyone—sorority girls and classics professors—unfortunate enough to be in their way.

CHAPTER SEVENTEEN

Always the Rebel

In a world where women are earthy and profane, she's the most foulmouthed, a virtuosa of vulgarity who makes me feel privileged when I walk into Farmer Jones's grocery for a hero sandwich, the line six deep with factory workers and grease-stained mechanics, and she looks my way and shouts, "Cocksucker, whaddya want!"

I loved her so much. Still do. She has red hair and drives a pink Cadillac. She skewers deadbeats whose scribbled IOUs stay overlong in the marbled notebook behind the counter while she spares the working poor.

"*Va a fancuolo!*" (Go fuck yourselves!) she barks with a grin as she waits for the Third Avenue light to change, saluting the *guaglione* on the corner and mocking the crones on the doorsteps fixing her with *il malocchio.* "Strangers in the Night" is blasting on the radio.

Lucy is tender with Cousin Margaret, the aging widow who now owns the store, but she happily exchanges the vilest profanity with Fat Rosie, a notorious gossip who spends fifty years on a chair on the sidewalk across from my house, and the tiny, titanically foulmouthed shopkeeper "Magala," cursing God and Jesus, all the saints, the born, the dead, and the not yet born. Even the wiseguys on Third Avenue who kill people can't handle this trio.

Lucy lives in a ground-floor apartment two doors down from Monte's Venetian Room where the food is Neapolitan and "Venetian," a sardonic reference to the Gowanus Canal down the street. Eddie Pole lives across the yard with his sons, Anthony Penguin and Johnny Boy, and daughters, Ginger and Cookie. Friday nights, the entire street cheers as the four siblings curse and pummel Eddie as he staggers home after blowing another paycheck in the Old Brigadier bar on Fourth Avenue.

Lucy lives at a time and a place where divorcées are branded sinners and whores by the *maldicenza,* though none dare say this to her face. Her mother, my grandmother, died when Lucy was a teen; her father, an immigrant fruit peddler, cannot understand his rebellious American daughter. When she's seventeen, Mike, a surly, leather-jacketed Brando-wannabe, roars across the Gowanus on a Harley and sweeps her off her feet. Three children later, he rides off, child support an alien notion. He runs a dimly lit bar on the far side of the Gowanus, while she struggles with abandonment, choking financial pressure, the terror of her children drowning in the tidal pull of the streets. She'll never, ever admit this.

On a summer evening, her eldest son shows up in tears at our door. "My father is drunk!" he says. "He's hurting her!" Joe is out the door in a flash, dodging traffic, running past crowded Monte's, my mother trailing behind.

"Joe, stop!" Gloria shrieks. "He could have a gun! Please!"

Once Joe gets going, nothing can stop him. Lucy is his baby sister. He gets to the car as it's pulling away from the curb, reaches inside the driver's window, grabs the gear selector, and jams it into PARK. The car jerks to a stop, knocking Joe on his ass. He's up in a flash. It's an unsettling thing to see my father and uncle, both wife beaters, flailing at each other in the gutter.

I babysit when Lucy works at Town & Country, the "World's Most Magnificent Nite Club" at the forgotten end of Flatbush Avenue. She wears skimpy outfits suited to women twenty years her junior, drinks with the wiseguys, makes connections. Her refrigerator is stocked with Genoa salami, *soppressata*, prosciutto, provolone, mozzarella, marinated mushrooms. The kids asleep, I play Gene Pitney ("It Hurts to Be in Love") over and over on her stereo until I'm trembling with emotion.

Next morning, when I show up, she overpays me, yelling, "Go out and get laid you dopey bastard!" And tosses me the keys to her new white Bonneville.

I head to Sunset Park hoping to glimpse Karen, a raven-haired girl I've met once. Another Sunday, teaching myself how to drive backward, I lose control and crash Lucy's Bonneville into my father's car, both vehicles insured in his name. Lucy lights a cigarette, coughs, and shrugs. I vanish before my father shows up. Honestly, at sixteen, I never imagine these two, my lodestars, are doomed.

Lucy and Fat Ernie's mom live across from one another. They waitress at Jean's Restaurant in Sheepshead Bay.

Tips are great and the "fell off a truck" swag—so much a part of life in Gowanus—is even better. A WWII widow, Maggie is plump, gregarious, psychotic. When she hears "niggahs on the roof," Lucy is there holding her, calming her, singing to her until the ambulance from Kings County Hospital's psychiatric ward pulls up and takes her away.

I show up at Jean's with my first date, a Jewish girl from Canarsie. When the rush slows, Lucy, who's piled our plates with shrimp; calamari; scungilli; hard, peppery *friselle*; and blistering red sauce, saunters over.

"Little prick!" she shouts. "Eating like you just got out of jail!"

I blush red as the sauce.

"*Madonna!*" a guy behind us bawls. "But you never change?"

"Your sister's ass!" she fires back.

"I don't got a sister!"

"Then go fuck *yourself!*"

Behind us, four wiseguys in silk shirts and razored haircuts, their *comare* (goo-mah) in tight skirts, melon breasts bursting out of blouses, sit at a table cluttered with platters of half-eaten shrimp, baked clams, whiskey glasses, ashtrays. They're drunk and laughing, but smoldering violence wafts off them like cheap cologne. Lucy nods at me, her "college kid nephew" which translates as "harmless idiot." One guy pulls a briefcase from under the table, snaps it open, and grabs a handful of delicate chains.

"Eighteen carat Italian," he says. "See for yourself."

Lucy saunters over. Busty, with thick hair, hanging earrings, and full lips, she resembles a rough-hewn Sophia Loren. She picks up a gold chain, examines it, and hands it to me. "Give this to your 'who-a' [whore] mother," she says grinning, knowing Gloria would never buy such an expensive trinket. She selects a pair of heavy gold earrings and bargains the price down to nothing, leaving the guy sputtering, his crew howling. She winks at me, hands the earrings to my date, and whispers something shameful in my ear.

✦ ✦ ✦

In the 1960s, Dyker Heights is a quiet, conservative, heavily Italian enclave a few miles from raucous Gowanus, notable for modest brick homes and over-the-top Christmas displays, a first stop on the road to suburbia. "My father won't even say 'damn,'" remembers my cousin Ann Marie D'Onofrio. Her mother, Frances, Lucy's older sister, says her prayers aloud kneeling by the side of her bed. On Sunday mornings, when the D'Onofrio family is getting ready for Mass at Our Lady of Guadalupe, Lucy shows up with pastry and pignoli cookies.

"How the fuck are you, cocksucker!" she greets my uncle Pat, a genial, straitlaced, family guy.

"The queen of cursing," remembers Ann Marie with a laugh. "Coming out of her mouth, it's poetry." Ann Marie's February birthdays—she's the only girl in a houseful of boys—are often canceled because of bad weather. "Lucy drives through snowstorms with three kids in tow to wish me 'Happy Birthday.'" The two, a generation apart, form a bond, Lucy sharing things she never discusses with anyone. "Tough as a tank on the outside, the hits just bouncing off, but she hides a ton of pain."

Holidays, Lucy arrives at family gatherings with pans of lasagna, a tower of fried shrimp, platters of antipasti. Summers, she drives her Cadillac, Lincoln, or whatever land yacht, to the far end of Coney Island near Sea Gate, the private, gated community. (Young Jeffrey Epstein is growing up there.) Lucy and her sisters chaperone a dozen nieces, nephews, stray adolescents she rounds up in Gowanus. They spread blankets on the hot sand, dip in the chill waters away from raucous, gang-ridden Bay 14. In her car, there are iced bottles of Manhattan Special, Brooklyn's legendary espresso soda, loaves of crusty Italian bread, pepper and egg omelets, salami sandwiches. The halcyon days stretch for years. "Eternal moments in our lives," as Ann Marie puts it.

No summer is endless. Few of these Gowanus kids live to see their thirtieth birthday. My younger brother Thomas is one of them. Born in a place where education is ignored, criminality encouraged, with scant awareness, desire, or a pathway into the larger world, they perish in a whirlpool of illness, poverty, violence, despair, dysfunction. In the eighties, a flood of brown Mexican heroin, distributed by the same wiseguys I considered heroes, piggybacks onto a terrifying new disease escaped from Central Africa. By their midteens, two of Lucy's three children are "chipping" heroin. Her daughter Lulu gets high with Johnny, the likable, Beatles-loving son of one of the neighborhood gangsters. Neither survives.

In Dyker Heights, Ann Marie and her three brothers are building stable lives and successful careers.

The midwife is a familiar figure in my grandparents' Gowanus. Half a century later, the abortionist, a specialist, is equally in demand. Lucy, in need of money, reaches out to connected guys. Soon, late night Caddies and Electras are gliding to and from the curb in front of

443 Carroll Street. Young women bundled in coats and scarves hurry into Lucy's apartment. Neighbors look the other way. Priests and police won't get involved. Gloria, very close to Lucy, is heartbroken.

"Lucy never overthinks anything," says Ann Marie. "She just acts and reacts." One afternoon, Sal and I find a bloody fetus in a paper bag in a trash-filled lot on the Gowanus. Looking back, I realize its significance.

Gowanus is still a place where the parish church is crowded with generations of families on Sundays, and children are dressed in the brown sackcloth of Saint Francis on October 4. My mother, struggling with faith, love, and perhaps a premonition of her own difficulties with my brother Thomas, reluctantly bars Lucy from our house, triggering furious battles with my father and outrage in me. In Dyker Heights Ann Marie hears her mother begging God "to forgive my sister for what she's doing."

✦ ✦ ✦

Lucy sees catastrophe coming, but escape, even at the practical level, requires cash, credit, cosigners, proof of income, almost impossible in the shadow economy she inhabits. When a house on middle-class Cortelyou Road in Flatbush comes available, she jumps, pulling her children Thomas and Lulu out of Gowanus. For the next years, she seemingly lives a normal life with a mortgage, a dog, and a boyfriend. But like the Prince in Poe's "Masque of the Red Death," Lucy doesn't realize Death is already in the room.

One afternoon, Thomas, Lucy's golden child, is beaten bloody in front of Monte's as the whole neighborhood watches. "He said the wrong thing to the wrong guy," a friend tells me, but Thomas, likable and loud, is strung out. Maybe he stole from unmerciful men, but just as likely he doesn't comprehend that the guys he grew up with must now be respected and approached with trepidation. Lulu, the little girl I babysat, has a daughter, Lara, born addicted to heroin. By age four, Lara knows to call Grandma if "something bad happens to Mommy." The gold *cornetto* amulet Lucy wears to ward off evil proves useless. "Imagine having two children addicts at the same time?" says Ann Marie.

Forced to sell the Cortelyou Road house, Lucy rents an apartment near Avenue X in Sheepshead Bay not far from Jean's Restaurant. My aunts beg her to turn over the proceeds for safekeeping. "Your children," Ann Marie remembers her mother pleading, "have taken so much already." She can't bring herself to do it. Instead, Lulu invites her latest boyfriend, a drug dealer, to move into the apartment, setting the final tragedy in motion. Lucy's cash, jewelry, the beloved furs hanging unworn in her closets are stolen and sold off. Like the pink Caddie that so impressed me as a boy, her possessions are tangible proof that Lucy lived life *her way*. Now, all is shading into despair and delusion. The kitchen where Lucy prepared sumptuous feasts—and six-inch-high lasagna—is littered with dirty syringes and spoons. Strangers clamor outside the door looking to score.

One afternoon, Lucy arrives home to find Lulu unresponsive on the pullout bed in the living room, arm thrust in the air as if beckoning, boyfriend long disappeared. Ann Marie rushes over, covers Lara's eyes, and carries the child outside. "My mom's dead, I know it!" Lara says over and over. She'll spend the next decades a runaway, a rebel, a wild child, trying to cope, sometimes failing.

Ann Marie sits with Lucy—Lulu stiffening with rigor mortis—until the medical examiner arrives and signs off. Lucy's feelings, memories, regrets, pain, as always, all locked inside her. Another devastating blow awaits. Getting high, Thomas shared needles with his Gowanus friends, certainly the vector that infects him with HIV. Asymptomatic for years, he enrolls in a methadone program, gets clean, meets and marries a neighborhood woman. He lands a job with Con Edison. Thomas tries to care for Lulu's daughter, Lara, but he's already a dead man. Delirious, in pain, wracked by waves of infection, in and out of hospitals, he dies in September 1994.

With this death, Lucy's fierce will fails. *Malocchio,* call it fate, myth, curse, or convergence, ultimately shatters her. She lives on, in failing health and with no resources. Ann Marie and her parents insist Lucy live in their basement apartment. "After all those years alone, she came to us," says Ann Marie. "Now it's her lungs, her legs, her loneliness." After 9/11, the world seemingly in flames, Lucy moves to an assisted living facility in Bay Ridge run by the Lutheran Church. The fierce redhead who never needs anyone or anything, who giddily told the world to "Fuck off!" is alone and afraid.

"Can you come?" she pleads with Ann Marie. "Can you come and see me?"

Aunt Lucy died more than twenty years ago. She's buried in Brooklyn's Green-Wood Cemetery, another unremarked grave, with her wayward children, Thomas and Lulu.

CHAPTER EIGHTEEN

My Friend Ray Sharkey

Ray Sharkey almost got away. A neighborhood guy who made it big in Hollywood, fled the desolation that dragged so many of us into early graves but couldn't escape the plague within. He was half Irish, with a long nose, sparkling eyes, pockmarked skin, and a voice like a rasp. He grew up in a row house across from Carroll Park, in the long shadow of the Gowanus Expressway. His father, a doorman, slipped out when Ray was five. His mother, Cecelia, pampered him, his *nonna* sang to him in Italian. You can see shards of his childhood, glittering and brittle, in Taylor Hackford's *The Idolmaker*, the film that won Sharkey the Golden Globe for Best Actor in a Motion Picture.

✦ ✦ ✦

Ray and I would walk together up to all-boys St. Augustine High School on Park Place. We walked along Union Street, past the apartment building where a Tuinal-enraged teen nicknamed "Boy-Boy" stabbed a Puerto

Rican to death for playing a guitar. Heads back, shoulders rolling, we'd stroll, wearing our purple-and-white letterman sweaters with the big *A* sewn above the pocket. Letters earned not on the field, court, or track but for pestering the dry, doddering, sinless Episcopalians who still dominated Park Slope into giving us cash in return for prayers, unnumbered and at unknown intervals, like Swiss bank accounts. One hundred dollars—my father earns less in a week unloading ships on the Red Hook piers—and the Christian Brothers name you a "centurion."

In a neighborhood where everyone—from Angioletti, the singsong fruit peddler, to the gamblers on the corner—shouts like a performer in some sidewalk opera, Ray is a loudmouth. Insecure, histrionic, attention starved, given to breaking out in a quavering doo-wop falsetto at a moment's notice. He's a few years younger than me, and he's best friends with my brother Joey. During the summer, Ray, Joey, and a short, curly-haired, granite-jawed football player named Raymond Bracco head to Brighton Beach; slather themselves with baby oil and iodine; smoke, ingest, and inhale every combination of alcohol and pharmaceutical; and roast themselves unconscious on teeny towels while trying to pick up Jewish girls from Ocean Parkway. I can still smell the salt tang and the sand cool under my feet in the boardwalk's shade.

Ray was part of the frantic gangbanger (South Brooklyn Boys, Bishops, Chaplains, Golden Guineas, Butler Gents) romantic-violent mix, a lost boy like my cousins Jimmy Psycho, JuJu, Popeye Anthony, and Richie Mel. He hung back, absorbed, observed, and seemed to master all the rage, pain, and hurt in the Gowanus ether.

Or so I thought.

Ray never finished high school, never was a centurion. He became an actor after seeing Jack Lemmon in *Days of Wine and Roses* (or was it *Hair*?) in Manhattan—that alien place we called the "City." Stories vary, but Ray knew his calling as surely as Saul of Tarsus was blinded by the light. He plunged into acting (inspiring my handsome and doomed brother Thomas), studying with Uta Hagen at HB Studio on Bank Street in Greenwich Village.

On a Sunday afternoon in the spring of '73, Ray shows up driving a Porsche 356—maybe one of the sports cars Philly Horse Teeth and Anthony Lips from Court Street steal and swap VINs with from wrecks rusting in Stuckey's Staten Island salvage yard. Stories differ. The *guaglione* gathered outside Monte's scratch their crotches, throw make-believe punches, laugh, dig the car. Ray basks in the attention. With him, a long-haired, bell-bottomed Puerto Rican Golden Gloves champ named Edwin "Chu-Chu" Malave looking to take his shot in Hollywood. Gloria serves platters of ravioli, meatballs, braciole, sausage, roast chicken, salad, and cannoli from Cioffi's on Union near Columbia Street. Homemade wine flows.

Ray entertains us with bits from *On the Waterfront* and *A Streetcar Named Desire.* He performs them on Brighton Beach with zinc oxide smeared on his nose. On Court Street, he's Stanley Kowalski outside the Off-Track Betting parlor. He begs Joey to come along ("Fuckin' California, man!"), but my brother is already passing into the limbo he'll inhabit for half his life. Gloria warns Ray to "be a good boy." He laughs a crazy laugh, clasps both hands to his temples.

"Stella-a-a-a!" he shouts.

And roars away.

I don't see Ray Sharkey for ten years. Word filters back to Gowanus when Ray Bracco visits LA: Sharkey is living on the beach in Malibu, film and TV offers pouring in. He's dating Italian actress Ornella Muti, a very beautiful woman. He's riding Harley-Davidsons with Sylvester Stallone and Gary Busey, draped in enough leather and chain to embarrass a Christopher Street fetishist. A strategic bandanna covers his thinning hair.

Somehow, I graduate from Columbia University's journalism school. I land a job with *Newsweek.* In 1982, the magazine's film critic David Ansen dispatches me to Los Angeles to profile this hot new movie star. My colleague David Friendly puts *me* up in the Beverly Hills Hotel. Ray has just won his Golden Globe. Critics are raving over his searing portrayal of Bob Marcucci, the man who loosed Fabian and Frankie Avalon on the world. Pauline Kael calls him "the next Jim Cagney." I never knew Cagney or Marcucci, but I recognize Ray Sharkey, the Ray thirsty for recognition and respect, leaking desperation like a sieve.

"Where's your brother?" he shouts when I arrive. "These neighborhood guys, they got a stupid apartment, they got a car, they're fucking some girl on the side. That's all there is to life? Tell him to get out here! I'll give him a job. He stays with me! No problem." He closes his fist and thrusts his thumb in the air like a guarantee. I know that gesture.

His life was changed but not transcended. Had he read his Chaucer at St. Augustine, Ray might have recognized the revelers in the "Pardoner's Tale" determined to triumph over death, might have remembered that long-ago Puerto Rican kid killed for playing a guitar. He's living with a slinky blond model. "Mienca, her family owns Kellogg's cereal!" he confides when we're alone, shaking his open hand like it's on fire. "You believe that shit?" Waiting to do my interview, I review his work: *The Idolmaker, The Lords of Flatbush, Who'll Stop the Rain, Willie & Phil, Miami Vice, Crime Story,* dozens of TV appearances, his characters trapped between violence and vulnerability.

"Yo, come with me," he says before I can start. This will be a pattern over the next days, my deadline clock tick-tick-ticking away. We drive, we eat Fatburgers, he buys a VCR—I've never seen one—and shows me more tapes. His characters tend to be named "Vinny." I like that. He'd finished *Some Kind of Hero,* a film about dysfunctional former POWs costarring Richard Pryor.

"*Madonna,* we spent a lot of time getting into character," Ray says.

For three days, he dances, he deflects, he feints and falls back on the old "dese and dose" tough-guy clichés. I don't have the heart or maybe the skill to press him. I have one brother dying of AIDS, another a junkie, a third an out-of-control gambler with wiseguys hot on his trail. I'm not making such smart life choices myself. Really, what could I ask him? His tight-lipped manager, Herb Nanas, only sees bigger successes. Giuseppe, his hairstylist, pronounces Ray "tan and fit," part of an unending spew of Hollywood hype. Other sources don't return my calls. My story is put on hold indefinitely.

Ray's twenty-nine years old. He has ten years to live.

✦ ✦ ✦

"I always knew I would fall—big-time," Ray tells my brother Joey in an unguarded moment. If anything, success accelerates his recklessness. Like so many who'd come of age along the Gowanus but with so much at his fingertips, Ray Sharkey has a four-hundred-dollar-a-day drug habit. Not coke, rampant in Hollywood, but heroin, straight out of the gutters and shooting galleries of Red Hook. Two marriages—to actors Rebecca Wood and Carole Graham—crumble under an avalanche of drug abuse. Car crashes and overdoses force him into monthslong rehab. When he relapses, starring roles give way to guest appearances, and even those rarely.

Summer 1992. Sharkey is in Vancouver to shoot an episode of a forgettable TV series. A suspicious package arrives. Customs inspectors alert police who discover heroin and cocaine in his hotel room. Ray is fired, the unforgivable sin in a business willing to look every other way. The impenetrable shield Hollywood extends over its own has cracked.

Ray isn't done yet. It's the age of AIDS, not Aquarius. Actress Elena Monica, daughter of comedian Corbett Monica, files an all-too-public lawsuit accusing Sharkey—who's lost forty pounds and can barely stand—of infecting her with HIV. To his shame, he stays in denial to the end, even after manager Herb Nanas reveals the truth. Ray returns to Gowanus to his mother. Tough as nails, Cecelia shields him to the very end. He passes away on June 11, 1993. Neighborhood people remember him as no more than "a wisp of dust."

I am reminded of Ray Sharkey in the summer of 2012 when I volunteer to write the script for a documentary on a historic Atlanta synagogue. The narrator turns out to be Tovah Feldshuh, who'd played Ray Sharkey's love interest in *The Idolmaker,* thirty years before. She's coming off a stint as Golda Meir in the long-running one-woman Broadway play *Golda's Balcony.* Of course, we talk about Ray. Tovah is one of those good-looking well-bred Jewish girls Sharkey would have loved to seduce.

And I wonder once again why our lives insist on unfolding the way they do. Tovah is married with grown children. She lives on Central Park West and grew up in affluent Scarsdale. Ray and I by the reeking Gowanus. Her father was an attorney. Ray's absentee father, a doorman; mine, a dockworker given to violent rages.

Is it destiny, nurture, nature, a chaos gene that selects for creativity and torment? Or the fact we lived in a self-contained world where teachers, police, clergy, and other authority figures were corrupt or uncaring, and Mafia guys our role models? It's all beyond my ken, save for the ache I feel when I remember Ray as he once was, as my brothers once were. For all his brilliance—and there is no question that Ray *was* brilliant—Sharkey sleeps in a lonely grave in a forgotten town on Long Island.

CHAPTER NINETEEN

Shooting Uncle Otto

At Otto's Social Club, the candy's stale and cigarettes cheap, smuggled tax-free from North Carolina. Uncle Otto (pronounced "Zee-ta-toe" in dialect) wears a suit, well cut, muted blue or brown, a white shirt and tie, and rarely speaks above a whisper, especially on the phone. Nearsighted, in his fifties, Otto might be an Allstate agent but for the gleaming Eldorado outside, his extravagant Christmas displays, and the rubber hose he uses to beat us when we're out of line.

My father's work clothes come from the dry goods store on Fifth Avenue, his tools twin wooden-handled baling hooks slung over his shoulder. For Otto's associates, sharkskin suits and pinkie rings connote savoir faire. When Otto's feeling good, he's laughing, joking, handing out Manhattan Special espresso sodas from the icebox like they're going out of style. He's the uncle I want.

Bookie parlors are raucous, aspirational like Pentecostal churches. Smoke chokes the air, gamblers lament, supplicants shout, debtors curse in tongues. Runners move in and out like wraiths. Otto takes bets from last-minute gamblers racing to ruination.

I have to hike to Park Slope to visit my doctor, but there are three bookie joints within two blocks of my house—Otto's on President Street, the Capri on Third Avenue, Nestor on Fifth Avenue, and even more on Court Street. On Smith, Joe Box makes book out of a walk-in refrigerator in Sam's Fruit Stand. On Henry Street, Jimmy the Mute wires his doorbell to a flashing light in his apartment not to miss a bet. On Fourth Avenue, Freddie "Blind Man" Monte hides bets inside the rubber ferrule of his cane. Fat Rosie runs a numbers operation from a metal folding chair in front of her house. Mornings, my mother and aunts pool their nickels and dimes, analyze their dreams over bitter coffee and pound cake, pray for riches. Rosie grows fatter.

Otto's is licensed as a social and athletic club, but the only athletics—football, baseball, and horse racing—blare on TV. There's a bocce ball court in the backyard, but no one ever plays. Uncle Otto doesn't even exist. He's Salvatore DeSimone, an oft-convicted felon. Even his building has a bad history—brawls, murder, corruption, dysfunction, and discord going back to the 1890s. In 1893, a dockworker is shot to death on Christmas Day. In 1894, a "banker" living there has his sixteen-year-old daughter jailed for vagrancy after a failed elopement. In 1956, "Otto," running the biggest policy bank in Brooklyn, flees after failing to bribe an undercover cop. In 1965, he's arrested again, as is his tough-as-nails wife when Feds break down her door. On the third floor, my neighbors' drug-addict son stabs his wife nineteen times in front of their toddler.

In Otto's back room, Peter, Ernie, Fishy, and I joke, curse, punch each other, eat sandwiches, play cards, mostly briscola and gin rummy for nickels and dimes. One afternoon, a pop-pop-popping pierces the drone of the television, then the shriek of tires. Outside, Otto's glasses are on the pavement; he's slumped to the ground, legs folded under like a ventriloquist dummy, blood spreading across his shirt. Women scream. Someone presses a towel to his side. Fishy, Otto's nephew, rushes him to Methodist Hospital. He survives. Next day, he's arrested *in his hospital bed.*

The Profaci family is warring with the Gallos. Otto, a Profaci, has been consorting with Crazy Joe Gallo. The Profacis are being taken over by the Colombos. It's all beyond me.

✦ ✦ ✦

Time passes. I'm a college student. On Third Avenue, two men I don't recognize spill out of Margie's bar, one cursing, red-faced, raging. Other guys stand in the entrance watching them. The angry one glances at me, blinks. I don't know if he's high, crazy, or drunk, but there's murder there. I turn, walk away, and keep walking. My family has lived here seventy years. My aunt *owned* the bar, and we lived next door. I was a school crossing guard on this same corner. What the fuck!

After college, I'm still hanging out in Otto's, when one Sunday, half a dozen guys in windbreakers burst through the door, shout, flash badges, rush the back room. (Like the Cheshire Cat, Otto has disappeared.) Federal agents and NYPD detectives acting on a tip instead find us eating meatball sandwiches. Threatening, cursing, arguing among themselves, they pound down the steps to the dank, low-ceilinged cellar, and then twenty minutes later stomp up and out the door.

Cops acting erratically is hardly news. One summer evening, four or five of us, guys and girls, stand on the sidewalk listening to Richie and Bobby Lombardi, sweet-voiced brothers, harmonize the Cadillacs' doo-wop classic "Gloria" when Blackie, the Irish beat cop, piles into us, nightstick at the ready, daring us to react. On Saturdays, I watch patrolmen from the 78th Precinct stroll into the Capri Club and emerge with a brown paper bag stuffed with cash. I've seen a patrol car chauffeur Mac, a hit man, around.

Three weeks later, the agents are back. This time with jackhammers, crowbars, and spades. In Otto's cellar, they dig up the bodies of a Colombo capo named Dominick "Mimi" Scialo and another unidentified male, both with bullet holes behind their ears.

The word is Scialo, ultraviolent and uncontrollable, was terminated by his own associates after he drunkenly insulted aging but formidable "boss of bosses" Carlo Gambino in a Coney Island restaurant. In another version, Scialo was seeing a shrink for anger issues, apparently an unforgivable sin among wiseguys. I'll never know—and don't want to know—if the wild-eyed guy who stumbled out of Margie's bar and froze my blood was Scialo.

Otto is dead. The building next door, once part of Otto's Social Club, now houses cityWell, a boutique bathhouse run by a woman who operates a "modern revival of the ancient tradition of the bathhouses in Rome, Greece, and Turkey." Her clientele are millennials, "likeminded wellness seekers in a nature-filled space." Where there were shouts, arguments, and gambling, there are now "luxurious" rain showers, aromatherapy, soaking tubs, a sauna, and a pergola, perhaps an unknowing nod to the Italians who came before.

Of course, she's never heard of Uncle Otto, his social club, or the corpses once rotting in the basement.

CHAPTER TWENTY

Crossing Flatbush

I'm seventeen years old. I've never kissed, never touched a girl. I can't do the Slop or the Locomotion. I did waltz with Jean W in Sister Mary Malachy's overblown production of Verdi's "La donna è mobile" at Our Lady of Peace's Christmas gala, an automaton in a cuckoo clock. I'm tired of walking eyes down along Con Edison's windowless brick wall on First Street while on the other side of the street, Lenny and Linda, Joe Bo and Dolores, and Larry and Christine moan softly in factory doorways.

Late one Friday night, five of us pile into Joey Formisano's white Grand Prix, lipstick-red interior reflecting my state of mind. Flatbush Avenue, with its outmoded men's shops, down-at-the-heels diners, sporting goods and army and navy stores, is the DMZ dividing the familiar—my house, my high school, the hospital where I was born—and the mysterious warren of crumbling brownstones that make up Fort Greene, Clinton Hill, Crown Heights.

I've seen a doomed United Airlines jet fall out of the

sky over Flatbush Avenue. I don't know it yet, but I will date a hot red-haired Sicilian who lives in a mansion next to the Grand Army Plaza arch until her father, a doctor, drives me away. This night, I've got thirty dollars in my dungarees, earned unloading tractor trailers stacked with leaky crates of Del Monte pineapple juice in nameless Long Island warehouses. We cross Flatbush at Bergen, passing the Pintchik Paints banner scrawled across the top floors of five buildings. TV sets glimmer in the windows. What is it like to live inside a sign?

In Neapolitan, Joey's nickname translates to "Shouldn't Happen to a Dog." Ernie, big as a pro wrestler, bursts into tears so often he's nicknamed "Niagara Falls." Frankie, a John Birch and Goldwater man, resembles a frog. Peter wears a toupee. I'm the bookish kid with fake front teeth. We're the guys they say "can't get laid in a whorehouse." We'll see.

Joey works in his father's Bed–Stuy fish market. Weekends, he shows up in Gowanus smelling of porgies and mackerel and is always out to have sex. This night, a customer has slipped him an address and a name of a "who-a" house on St. Marks Avenue. We're off.

After fifteen minutes, I realize we've circled Fort Greene Park and Brooklyn Tech three times, never knowing that once you cross Flatbush, streets can literally change names. When Joey stops at a light, I lower the passenger window. Two young guys are standing on the corner.

"Excuse me . . ."

"Don't ask them!" Ernie hisses.

"Why not?"

"What you need, baby?" the taller one says, walking

over. He's wearing eye makeup and a do-rag like a pirate in *Peter Pan.*

"I got what you need," he says, wagging his tongue obscenely.

The second guy, a thin-mustachioed Little Richard look-alike, strolls over in a cloud of perfume and taps the rear window. Ernie looks straight ahead; he's constantly teased for having bigger breasts than any girl in Gowanus.

"Got smoke [marijuana], Reds, Johnnie Walker, a crib for y'all white boys to party," he drawls, jerking his thumb toward a brick row house just off the corner, music blasting. Through the first-floor windows I see Black men gyrating to Martha and the Vandellas' "Dancing in the Street." Two more men walk up to our white car, more perfume, long scarves, and processed hair.

"Where the ladies?" Joey says, leaning across the console.

The pirate's mouth twists sourly. "Ladies? Shit! Don't need no . . ." He pauses. "Ladies in the kitchen, sugar. Park and I'll show you."

"How we get to St. Marks?" Joey asks, handing the guy a few crumpled dollars.

"Fuck I know!" the pirate says. "Ain't nothing bitches do I ain't do!" He stomps off.

There's this relationship between the flamboyant homosexuals of Gowanus and the macho street guys. One Saturday, Sarah and Sally, hairdressers and sometime drag queens, invite us to a party near Brooklyn Heights, another world to me. As always, they make it sound seductive and outrageous; we pretend to believe them. The Hicks Street building overlooking the BQE is so ancient, the stairwells are outside the walls. Five of us climb up, fighting through a barrage of soul music. The door is wide open. Inside, it's hot and crowded. Candles stuck in Chianti bottles the decor. In one bedroom, older men and boys writhe like a bundle of snakes. I don't stay long. Some guys do.

✦ ✦ ✦

Next stop, a row of bars near the Brooklyn Navy Yard. During the war, seventy thousand sailors, shipbuilders, engineers, stevedores, and civilian workers, Gloria and her girlfriends among them, worked at the yard. Things have slowed dramatically. Papa John's tavern is on its last legs, still run by an uncle I know as "Schnozzle Durante." Schnozzle cheated on Aunt Josie, my mother's older sister, and earned the undying enmity of the six Giordano sisters. For the rest of her life, the woman he cheated with and married is "the who-a."

Smokey Robinson's "The Tracks of My Tears" blasts from the jukebox. The place smells of spilled beer and stale cigarette smoke. A sad-looking man in a Perry Como jacket and a few bleary merchant sailors are clumsily dancing with young disinterested girls. I cringe, seeing myself in twenty years. The five-dollar shot of cheap rye whiskey I gulp makes me nauseous.

Joey makes the call from a pay phone by the toilets. We stand around, gaping. He nods, grins, hangs up, and waves. I'm out the door, Schnozzle Durante and his betrayal forgotten.

✦ ✦ ✦

Midnight at St. Marks Avenue. It's a residential street, deserted, except for one brownstone, light seeping through the parlor floor curtains. Joey parks the Grand

Prix—it stands out like Moby-Dick—and we head up the long block giggling and slapping each other in the head, shouting, "Shit's on!" I've no idea what to expect. My notion of a whorehouse is tinkling pianos, Miss Kitty, the Long Branch Saloon.

I'm Cinderella with midnight approaching. Joey flies up the stoop, hits the doorbell, Peter, Frankie, and Ernie right behind him. An unwanted notion has popped into my head, maybe from reading too many books: romance, love, sex are entwined and inseparable, like doo-wop music, fading but still potent. Last summer at Paradise Park, a freckled blonde named Trish, a friend of my cousin Clementine, slipped into my bedroom and hid a hand-drawn paper heart under my pillow. I hadn't really noticed Trish, but her gift sent a wave of heat through me.

At a party at the Rip Van Winkle Lake boathouse that night, Trish, in tight leopard-print pedal pushers, drunkenly tried to push me onto a blanket—a few times. I was finally getting the point when a fifteen-year-old named George, a head shorter than me, walked up and shouted, "Trish is my girl. Leave her alone!" He was trembling, whether in rage or fear, but I heard him.

The brownstone's glass-paneled double doors open, and half a dozen frat boys in madras shirts, penny loafers, and khakis pour out, giggling. They head noisily down the street. An attractive woman in her forties stands in the doorway.

"Is Jackie home?" Joey says (like an idiot).

She frowns, looks us over.

"Ricky told us to ask for Jackie," Joey adds. "He gave

me this address . . ." He pulls a crumpled strip of brown paper—something he'd maybe wrapped fish in—out of his pocket. "You know, Ricky from the fish store on Broadway?"

"Don't know no Ricky."

"We just talked on the phone!" Frankie says.

Apparently deciding we're harmless, she steps back. I follow them into a pine-floored, high-ceilinged foyer, a wide oak door on the right, staircase on the left. Plaster angels smile down from the ceiling, a stained-glass panel over the transom. Faded, in disrepair, the place is nicer than anything in Gowanus. Jackie is all business. "Twenty dollars for twenty minutes," she says. "No rough stuff, no drugs, no drinking. Pay me now. Tips is extra."

I'm last, pulling wrinkled bills out of my pants, handing them over. She counts carefully, then slides the parlor door open. We pile in, then line up along the wall like Catholic schoolboys in a spelling bee. Six girls lounge on sofas and mismatched upholstered chairs watching TV, oblivious to us. Dressed in low-cut sweaters, loosely tied nightgowns, halters, tight pants, short-shorts. Everything is spilling out, and I can't stop staring. It's like a song Murray the K plays endlessly on WINS—"short ones, tall ones, fine ones, kind ones."

Joey, Peter, and Frankie step up, grab three busty women off the sofa, and head for the staircase. Suddenly, it's quiet, so quiet, I think I hear the steps moan under Ernie's weight. Across a coffee table cluttered with ashtrays, Chinese takeout, and Coke cans, a skinny girl in a pale blue blouse stares vacantly at the television. She's pretty, much younger than the others, her backstory already spooling in my head: she's sad, scared, distracted, distraught (bored never occurs to me). I know I should be raunchy, horny, lustful, libidinous, but life is always more vivid in my imagination.

Time passes, then doors open and close, stairs creak, a baby cries somewhere, a toilet flushes, voices buzz. The front door opens. I approach her.

"I'm Vinny," I mumble.

She says nothing, gets up, takes my hand, and walks me up the staircase, her hand rough to my touch. At the top, she steps into a small bedroom. A big bed, oak dresser, and a clock. She pulls down a chenille bedspread, turns toward me, steps out of her pants, reaches behind to unhook her bra.

It's happening too fast.

"Wait," I say. "What's your name? You from Brooklyn?"

She looks at me for the first time. "Odette. I'm from Ka-lina. Jackie my aunt." It sounds like "ahnt." She speaks with a soft drawl, instantly carrying me back to a South I've never seen and can't imagine.

"Let me."

She shrugs, drops her hands, turns her back to me. I step forward, unhook her bra, cup her small breasts. Not sure what to do next, I run my hands over her belly, startled by the raised edge of a horizontal scar. I've heard the old men, many WWII vets, playing gin rummy and pinochle in the Glory Social Club, argue whether Asian girls have sideways boxes. Sounds stupid. Black girls? I'm about to find out . . .

"That my baby scar."

"Oh."

"Got fifteen minutes left," she says, pulling away.

"I . . ."

"You can do a half and half."

"Half and half?"

She walks me over to the bed, unzips my pants, starts jerking me in and out, her hands like sandpaper, nearly catching my dick on my zipper. In twenty seconds, I know we're not getting to the next half.

"Stop, okay. Stop."

She shrugs, lets go.

A wave of shame, bright red, passes over me.

I'm one of four boys. I've never seen a vagina. I've heard a hundred jokes, know the word in English and Neapolitan slang. In Honey's basement, I watched a blurry black-and-white movie about a French nun. When the nun pulls off her habit, even squinting, all I can see is a bird's nest running halfway down her thigh.

"Pull 'em down," I say, trying to stir myself.

She looks at me, does nothing.

"Here." I pull the last five bucks out of my pants. "Here."

She rolls the top of her panties down, sways her hips, then drops them to her knees. I stare, stepping closer. My hands ache to touch her.

Down the hall, a baby cries forlornly. It breaks my heart.

"You gots to go," she says.

The Grand Prix is idling by the curb. I open the passenger door. Peter gets out, pounds me on the back.

"You did it!"

The rest of them are laughing, high-fiving, shouting over each other. I slip into the back seat.

"Great, right?" Joey says. "Told you!"

"Fucking A!"

Actually, "Fucking D," I think.

Maybe worse. The locusts already nibbling in my head—Immaturity, Insecurity, Impotence—will take years to dislodge. When we recross Flatbush at Bergen, I notice the TVs in Pintchik's wall are dark. Somehow, it's two a.m. Joey drives to the twenty-four-hour Neergaard on Seventh Avenue. We get out.

Now what?

The drugstore is empty. A clerk reads a newspaper on the counter.

"We need five Pro Kits," Joey says. The guy looks up and walks to the back.

"What's that?"

"You'll see," he says, grinning.

The clerk returns with a handful of thick crinkled envelopes. Black lettered labels, exactly like the government surplus junk I find in army and navy stores.

"Ten dollars plus tax."

Peter slaps twenty dollars on the counter. "Keep it," he tells the bewildered druggist. Peter is like that.

In the back seat, I squint to read the label, *Emergency Prophylactic Treatment Kit.* It's dated 1944. We sit silent as Joey drives to Third Street and Bond, a grim strip of factories and abandoned warehouses abutting the Gowanus.

We get out of the car; by now, it feels like the hundredth time. I tear open the envelope. Inside, there's a cleansing cloth, a cotton sack with a drawstring, a tube of sulfathiazole ointment with a long, screw-on snout like an anteater.

We stand in a rough half circle around Joey. He unzips his pants, pulls out a wrinkled uncircumcised penis.

"Motherfucker!" Frankie exclaims.

"Gotta use these or get gonorrhea or the sift," Joey says.

I won't, but I don't say it.

Joey removes the cap on the ointment tube, screws on the extension, inserts it into his penis, and twists. Once, twice.

"Ahhhh!" A collective moan.

We stand there in pain in the middle of the night, in the gutter, twisting and twirling.

Two years will pass before I lose my virginity. It happens in the basement of my girlfriend's house in Canarsie, her parents upstairs watching *Get Smart.*

CHAPTER TWENTY-ONE

Swimming to Forever

The moment Joe and Gloria head out to do Saturday shopping, Joey grabs a wooden kitchen spoon and pounds away on three dented aluminum pots. In the bathroom, I spill bottles and jars from the medicine cabinet, throw open the window, stare across a spiderweb of clotheslines, and begin my latest experiment. Thomas disappears into our parents' bedroom. Twenty minutes later, Joey and I sit transfixed by *The Lone Ranger* when Thomas bursts through the French doors.

"A fiery horse with the speed of light, a cloud of dust, and a hearty Hi ho, Silver!" he shouts.

He's wearing Gloria's high heels, pearls, a smear of red lipstick. Prancing around, exaggerating our mother's sashaying until we're hysterical, he then vanishes into the bedroom to change before Joe gets back. The memory is still vivid when I visit Joe, Gloria, and Thomas, asleep in a shared grave in Green-Wood Cemetery.

✦ ✦ ✦

I love my brothers, allies and victims in the long war Joe wages on his family. Joey, four years younger than me, is athletic; I'm bookish. At ten, Thomas, already a mirror reflecting beauty, innocence, and illusion, is a boy who never hesitates to sacrifice his child's milk-white body on those appalling nights when Joe beats our mother. The animal lover on a street where other kids tie strings of firecrackers to cats' tails, who moves to Greenwich Village and rides the subway into Brooklyn on Easter morning, a cardboard box of chirping ducklings and chicks under his arm, and convinces Gloria, who loves him best, to tend to them. Where he gets them is always a mystery. As a teen, Thomas's sunny disposition clouds into uncertainty when a tumor in his leg and parathyroid surgery scar him like a victim in a slasher film. The chicks and ducklings are eaten by backyard rats.

I have three dozen first cousins, more tribe than family. Thomas is always the center of things, laughing and teasing and joking at Sunday spaghetti dinners; at his First Communion, chubby face atop a white suit; at Paradise Park, our extended family's funky but beloved getaway in the Catskills, catching frogs in the creek, belting off-key doo-wop songs to cousins Donna Garrison, Louise, Fran, and Clem Abatemarco.

At Our Lady of Peace School, all the girls in their tartan jumpers have crushes on him. Old Italian ladies look at him wistfully. Boys are uncertain. Thomas doesn't care about wiseguys, sports, or gambling, pillars of Gowanus culture. He doesn't drive, the lessons on Joey's stick-shift VW aborted when our irascible father bites Thomas's knee. Never teased like Butchie, the school crossing guard who flaunts a scarlet streak in his hair. Joe Coppola is too volatile for anyone to dare.

Masculine and sensitive are discordant. A day comes when the son of a wiseguy taunts Thomas, a few thugs egging him on. Thomas can't "handle himself," but he's got our prizefighter grandfather's pugnacity and our father's short fuse. In seconds, the instigator is on the sidewalk, Thomas flailing away.

"Leave the kid alone!" a guy shouts. "You're gonna hurt him!"

The fight becomes a neighborhood legend.

At Brooklyn College, Thomas meets Pam, a tall, blue-eyed Norwegian from Bay Ridge; together, they make an otherworldly couple. Strolling from the Union Street subway station on Sundays, she clings to him so tightly, Fat Rosie shouts an obscenity; the other gossips put down their knitting. The *guaglione* are speechless. Pam's cousin visits from Long Island; I cling to her, but nothing comes of it.

I marry Adrienne, my second girlfriend. She and Thomas are best buddies. Sunday afternoons, I'm watching football; they're shopping in the West Village. Thomas, she notices, is popular on Christopher Street.

Thomas meets Ray Sharkey at our family's Sunday dinner. Mesmerized, he watches Ray, pure talent and jittery energy, do impromptu bits at our dining room table. Sharkey's leap from Gowanus to Hollywood must seem unimaginable. Glorious Foods, the city's toniest caterer, hires Thomas as one of their stunning cater waiters. Suddenly, it's crystal goblets and sconces at the Met, celebrity soirees in the Hamptons. Fashionistas, financiers, photographers, designers, and the rich and bored toy with him. Thomas doesn't understand he's on the menu. Later,

I suspect he doesn't care. One day, I'll find an engraved invitation from a British blue blood inviting him to London. Thomas makes the trip.

He lives in a walk-up at 187 Bleecker Street at the corner of MacDougal, a turn-of-the-century tenement smelling of garlic and simmering tomato sauce. Joe, Gloria, Joey, and I help with the move. I remember gasping as I lug boxes up endless stairs; his neighbors, black-clad *nonnas* who've lived in the building forty years, zip past with shopping bags of groceries. I remember how they cry when he dies.

Friends tell me the apartment is a "clubhouse" where Thomas re-created the childhood he wanted, open to all, including a hairless stray cat named Chance. Forty years later, Violetta Filippone, an Italian fleeing a bad marriage, remembers Thomas giving her a place to stay. "You could see the World Trade Center from his window." Café Reggio is across the street. HB Studio, where Ray Sharkey got his start, is a few blocks away.

It's 1979. Thomas is a model. One gig has him in bed with a gorgeous woman in Bergdorf Goodman's window. Half our family shows up to wave. He's a member of a ragged revival of *Hair* touring inner-city neighborhoods on a flatbed trailer. Auditioning, taking acting and dancing classes. On Sundays, Easter chicks and ducklings give way to peacocks: Roy Reid, an acclaimed ballet dancer from Zimbabwe; photographer Carmine Schiavone, whose work appears on the covers of *Cosmopolitan* and *Vogue*; Jo-Ann DiLorenzo, a makeup artist who works with Van Halen and Talking Heads; Dawn Wolf and Denise Rothstein, feisty jazz musicians' daughters who'll stand by Thomas until the end; and artist Joel Sokolov, who

On the Town. Joe and Gloria before he shipped out to the Pacific.

Al Fresco. Thomas, Joe, Vincent, Joe Jr., and Gloria, all dolled up for Sunday sidewalk dinner at the Giordano house.

Coppola Sisters. Left to right: Tessie, Rosanne, Frances, and Lucy (in fur).

Coppola Family. Top, left to right: Vincenzo, Anna, Tessie, Zia Alfonsina, and Zio Tomasso Tramontano. Bottom, left to right: Joe, Rosanne, Frances, Lucy, and cousin Mariuchelle.

(BELOW) *Coppola Cousins. Top, left to right: Joey Coppola and Michael Giovannuci. Middle, left to right: Thomas Giovannucci, Anthony Siconolfi, and Angelo Siconolfi. Bottom, left to right: Vincent Leonti and John D'Onofrio. Foreground: Thomas Coppola waving.*

Joe Coppola. He stole, then squandered, Gloria's heart.

Giordano Family. Top, left to right: Great-uncles John, Timsey, and William. Middle, left to right: Anthony, Jimmy (my grandfather), great-aunt Rose, Frank, and Louis. Front, left to right: great-grandmother Josephine and great-grandfather Salvatore Giordano.

Plumbing the American Dream. Great-uncle Anthony Giordano in a T-shirt with infant son and future New York Supreme Court justice Anthony Jr. in his wife Filomena's arms.

Gowanus Rising. Long-abandoned transit powerhouse, since reborn as Powerhouse Arts Center.

The Beast in the Basement. Half a century later, Brother Masseo Butteri's sexual abuse is still coming to light.

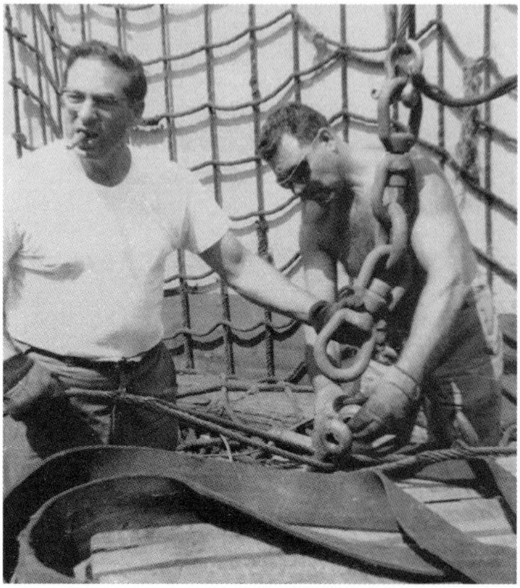

On the Docks. Uncle "Big Sonny" Giordano (with cigar), a polestar in my life.

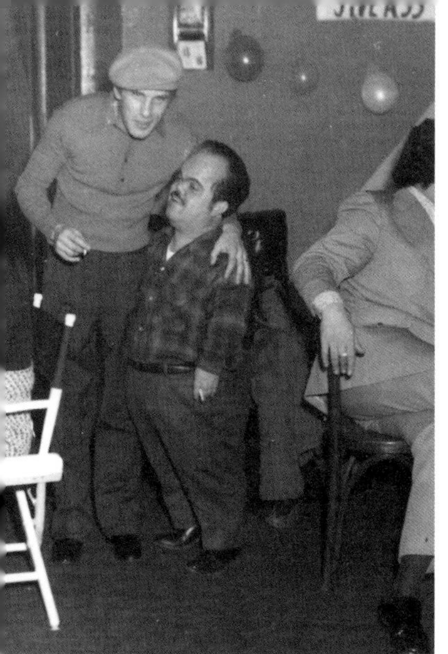

De-Capo-Tated. "Crazy" Joe Gallo and Armando "the Dwarf" Illiano partying at the Gallo headquarters, 51 President Street.

Partners in Crime. Hugh "Mac" McIntosh and Carmine "Junior" Persico (in foreground).

Garfield Boys at the 78th Precinct. Hauled in after a teen is shot to death in a 1950 Prospect Park gang fight. On left, Anthony "Scappy" Scarpati. Second from right, future Colombo boss Carmine "Junior" Persico. Scarpati pleaded guilty to manslaughter and received a fifteen-to-thirty-year sentence. After his release, Persico promoted Scarpati to captain. Both men died in prison.

Pompadours and Skinny Ties. Top left: Fat Ernie. Bottom, left to right: Joey "Elvis" Barbella and Richie Lombardi.

Paradise Park. Gloria, me (wearing cool army belt), Joe, and Aunt Lucy.

Boys' Night at Coney Island. Top, left to right: Lenny, Joe Bo, me, Fishy, Peter, and Joey Formisano. Bottom, left to right, Dennis Pots, Frankie Garofalo, Barry (a future Green Beret), Fat Ernie.

Gowanus's Last Gasp. Glory Social Club before its December 2024 demise. Generations of neighborhood men argued, gambled, and played cards there. Another victim of gentrification.

All My Trials. Cousin Richie in an orange jumpsuit arguing one of his cases.

Thomas Coppola. My beautiful, doomed younger brother.

embroiders my brother's name—position 39A—on the AIDS Memorial Quilt.

They pile out of taxis dressed like gypsies, Thomas in a black leather trench coat, long scarf, boots, and cowboy hat, bearing exotic flowers, truffles from Manhattan's best chocolatiers, cannoli from Veniero's Pasticceria. Gloria and Joe, who spend hours preparing these dinners, couldn't be more delighted. Thomas is delivering the world to their door.

One weekend, Adrienne and I catch the ferry to Fire Island at the absolute peak of the throbbing Donna Summer "I Feel Love" moment. Thomas, whose friends have a place at the Pines, treats us royally, takes us to dinner, gives up his room. Beautiful men drag Adrienne onto the Ice Palace disco floor.

Next morning, on Cherry Grove Beach, Thomas, who's been hitting the gym, stands there, sun-bleached hair and rippling muscles. He grins at me under his crazy-long eyelashes and dives into the surf. He swims and swims—I can't even dog paddle—until he's nothing more than a dot on the painted ocean, until I'm terrified he'll die or swim to forever. Finally, he turns around and slowly heads back to shore.

CHAPTER TWENTY-TWO

Margie

We live above a bar once owned by Zia Alfonsina on Third Avenue and Carroll. Weekends, I'm jolted awake by breaking glass, howls of pain, shouted imprecations, and threats in unfamiliar languages. The loudest, most ferocious voice is female.

"*Levati dal cazzo!*" ("Stay the fuck out of here!") Margie bellows.

From our kitchen window, I watch two drunks pick themselves out of the gutter and stagger toward the waterfront. They're merchant sailors, bewitched by the siren song of the hooker bars near the Navy Yard, only they've lost their way and stumbled into a creature who'd make a Cyclops blink, a woman with a wrestler's bulk, a swirling Prince Valiant hairdo, and murder in her heart.

Margie, the bar's most recent owner, is a familiar, even friendly figure in the neighborhood. Granted, she doesn't walk; she swaggers, has a hair-trigger temper, and a mouth that rivals my aunt Lucy's epic vulgarity. She also holds an MA in English literature.

My friend Joe Bo, a family member, once asked, "Ma, is Margie a girl?"

"Margie is married! She's got a husband!"

"Mom, she beats the shit out of men!"

Margie is not a woman to worry about whose laundry is the whitest.

Like me, Margie is from an old Gowanus clan. She was born into a place where disdain for rules, roles, expectations, authority is a virtue. Like me, her early role models are gangsters. At the same time, she's demonstrably, even obstinately, religious. She goes to Mass, donates generously to church charities, "adopts" a young refugee—word has it, a nun. Her father is a loan shark, and her uncle a button man. Her mother likes to don a bathing suit and frolic under a blasting fire hydrant on President Street with kids fifty years her junior.

Conflicted?

By night, Margie runs her bar. Carmine "Junior" Persico, dapper Gennaro "Gerry Lang" Langella, and fearsome Hugh McIntosh hold a special place in her heart. She visits Langella, convicted of racketeering and extortion, as he's about to disappear for one hundred years in federal prison. Dozens of neighborhood characters, Chitty, Blubberhead, Freddie Fish, Al Potato-King, Muzzi, and Funzi, are regulars in Margie's bar. I go there for meatball sandwiches. She hires go-go girls to perk up business, then threatens to beat the fuck out of any guy who dares hit on them.

By day, Margie teaches at John Jay High School on Seventh Avenue. Her approach to discipline is in line with Sister Mary Malachy and the Christian Brothers who terrorize my high school. She's friends with my college-educated, muscle-bound cousin Johnny Pomarico, a lieutenant in the NYPD's intimidating Tactical Patrol Force. Through Johnny, Margie takes an interest in me, a bookish student in a place where "book" usually means "take a bet." My NYPD uncles want me to work in the Department of Sanitation. "Great benefits!"

"Don't pay them any mind!" Margie growls. "They're all morons!"

✦ ✦ ✦

This Friday night Joe Bo and I are huddled in the back of her speeding sedan, no idea where we're headed. Maybe Coney Island for Nathan's hot dogs? Over the Brooklyn Bridge to West Third Street, where there's a gay dance club, the Tenth of Always? Margie says Andy Warhol is a regular, though I've never heard of him. In Greenwich Village, the Mafia and the vice squad are a tag team, harassing and shaking down hapless homosexuals.

Instead, Margie, her forearm like Popeye's, cuts across three lanes of traffic on Hamilton Avenue, not a care in the world. Horns blare as we cross into dangerous Red Hook. She parks outside a crumbling warehouse—my father works two blocks away—and raps on a metal door with a ring of car keys.

The gatekeeper, seeing a dragon at his door, gives way.

Masked by a clouds of cigarette smoke, dozens of shouting, jostling men, schemers, petty criminals, desperate gamblers arrived straight from the track, car service drivers, shopkeepers, my Klor-Dee dry cleaner, are standing, squatting, praying, cursing, as a high-stakes crap game unfolds.

Margie, the only woman in the room, nods at the guy

running the game and wades in, a fistful of twenty-dollar bills in her hand. (Joe and I fade into the background.) She elbows her way to the craps table. No one says a word, not even when she constantly bets against the shooters. An hour later, a scrum of drunks and losers is glaring at us. Red Hook is a murderous place. It strikes me: Margie is not fearless; she's nuts.

I'm in journalism school when next we meet. Margie is writing a book. I'm transfixed, imagining the tales she'll tell. When she meekly asks if I'd edit her book, I jump. When it finally arrives, it's my elementary school Baltimore catechism come to life: hundreds of pages of prayers, religious devotions, saints' lives, Mariolatry, rosary mysteries. Not a single personal detail or anecdote. I duck her for months.

One day, word spreads: Margie has lost her teaching job at John Jay. This is a Gowanus hero: college grad; educator; takes no shit from punk kids, whiny parents, or cowardly administrators. Worse, she's been fired, a very rare thing. In my four years teaching in public schools, I've watched staggering drunks gulp whiskey in the back of classrooms. In Bushwick, I somehow miss a student climbing out my second-story window. I never fear; our fanatical teachers' union president, Albert Shanker, is there. "When schoolchildren start paying union dues," he insists, "that's when I'll start representing the interests of schoolchildren."

Even Al Shanker can't save Margie. Her crime: She bit a student in the head.

And that's how I remember her.

CHAPTER TWENTY-THREE

Pots at the Bay Au Go-Go

Pots was always the odd man out, a German blond sweet-faced, corn-fed-looking teen dropped among swarthy and rambunctious Italians. No drunk or dope fiend, no menace to society, yet he's the first of us to be homeless. His father is an NYPD detective; his mother, a beautician from Tennessee who dyes her hair blue decades before it's fashionable. They toss him out like a bundle of rags on his eighteenth birthday.

He tumbles out of middle-class Park Slope into turbulent Gowanus, a high school dropout with Vietnam looming and little hope for deferment. No troublemaker or athlete, Pots entertains us with lurching, groaning Frankenstein imitations in John Sanseverino's candy store on Carroll Street. Augie Aversano, a head shorter and bowlegged, accompanies him playing Igor's imaginary flute.

Pots is also the guy who never knows when to stop. Not when elderly John and his wife, Jenny, are apoplectic, not when third graders from Our Lady of Peace School hoping to buy lunch-hour red licorice, candy corn, and Squirrel Nut Zippers flee the store in tears. Addicted to surf music, hot rod cars, and not much else, Pots takes a job working nine p.m. to five a.m. at California Pies on Douglass Street figuring he'll eat free, save money, and avoid paying rent. Shift over, he's back on Carroll Street at six a.m.

In 1966, I'm at Brooklyn College, dating Laura, my first girlfriend, who lives in faraway Canarsie. I don't have a car and get home at three a.m. Three hours later, Pots knocks on our front door.

"Is Vinny coming out?"

Who wouldn't come out at six a.m. on a Sunday morning?

He's already tried Ernie a few doors down. Ernie, appearing like an obese Lee Harvey Oswald at his second-floor window, blasts away with a Daisy BB rifle, driving the hapless Pots, whooping and hollering, up the street.

A saint of the afflicted, Gloria invites him in for breakfast. By now, my father is halfway through his first pack of Luckys, the second of many pots of bitter Savarin coffee, and is studying the *Racing Form* with the intensity of a Talmud scholar.

"Vinny, Pots is here."

"Mom," I croak. "Please." I bury my head in my pillow, but it's no use.

"Vinny, your friend is here!"

The edge in my father's voice is a clear signal. Instantly, I'm wide-awake and out of bed. My brothers are sleeping down the hall, so I still have time for my weekend commando raid. Joey is my size, Thomas close but more stylish. I tiptoe into the front bedroom and scoop up whatever jeans, tees, sweaters, or sneakers I figure I'll need for the day, then dart back to my tiny room. A moment later, big work boots clump on the staircase, and the cheap knob on the hollow wooden door rattles.

"Vinny?"

I slither into a pair of Joey's bell-bottom Seafarers. Pots stomps in with the grace of a Harryhausen stop-motion creature.

"There you are!" he says, grinning. "Your mother's looking for you. She's making ham and eggs!" My mother is downstairs, twelve feet away.

"Great," I mutter.

Saturday mornings, the police; Cousin Jimmy Pomarico and Uncle Sonny Boy Giordano, the dockworkers; Cousin Jerry Pepe and Uncle Big Sonny Giordano, the tightly wound gamblers; Frankie Masters; and Uncle Punchy all show up at our door either going to or getting off work, eager to handicap the day's card at Aqueduct. Sometimes my classmate Butchie Mulia, a handicapper from Sixth Street, shows up. Instantly, Joe Coppola becomes the doting father I never see.

The ritual has been ongoing at our house for years with the same cast of characters. It begins civilly with small talk about wives and kids, and then it's down to business, a debate triggered by an item in horse-racing bibles, *The Morning Telegraph* and the scratch sheet. Last night, my father sent Thomas to the newsstand on Union and Fourth Avenue, but the few copies of the *Telegraph* had already been grabbed by hardcore gamblers who stood waiting for the delivery truck. As vain and lackadaisical as he is handsome, Thomas saunters over to Ninth Street, two moonstruck girls on his arm, and then, feeling a little edgy, on to the Prospect Avenue station, literally following the RR subway line into

Bay Ridge. No luck. In full panic, he rushes back to the Pacific Street station, on a corner thick with pimps and junkies, and gets the papers.

At the table, the talk is weight and track conditions and supposed tips from the trainers and jockeys, but jittery, contrarian Jerry Pepe, who cannot speak below a roar, soon has everyone enraged and shouting.

"Moron!"

"Imbecille!"

"Stronzo!"

My father's go-to insult in these years is "morphadite!" Where he picked up "hermaphrodite" among the sacks of coffee in the hold of a cargo ship, I'll never know. This happens as steaming pots of coffee, fried eggs, slices of Boar's Head Deluxe Ham, buttered baguettes delivered still hot moments before from Gallo's Bakery come marching out of Gloria's tiny kitchen.

Looking back, these are among the happiest memories of my life.

✦ ✦ ✦

The Gowanus of my youth is still crowded with oddballs and characters decades after the first waves of Italian immigrants escaped to Long Island, Staten Island, and New Jersey. Ernie's father died in World War II, so he acts out by stealing Cadillacs and Continentals from Monte's parking lot while patrons, some of whom are mafiosi, are dining. Joe Duck, the attendant, no genius, leaves the keys in a little booth outside the restaurant. Ernie also drives his silver Plymouth GTX through a crowded Italian *feste* while Anna Fantasia and some lecherous greenhorn musicians are onstage singing and dancing the tarantella.

"La, la, la, fried fish and baccala!"

Ernie's mother—Honey's sister—hears "niggahs on the roof" of her wood-frame house. When she's hysterical, an ambulance appears, lights flashing, outside her door. Cops and EMTs hasten inside—a familiar routine on Carroll Street—and take her howling to Kings County Hospital as we look away. In a few weeks, she's back at Jean's Restaurant in Sheepshead Bay fixing heaping bowls of spicy spaghetti and clams for Ernie, Pots, and me.

✦ ✦ ✦

The Bay Au Go-Go is around the corner from Jean's, but the reception couldn't be less welcome: Seemingly minutes after we arrive, Pots is clinging by his fingertips to the rear window of Joe Bo's accelerating car, blood streaming down his battered face. Ernie is holding on next to him, trailed by a dozen howling bartenders, bouncers, waiters, busboys, cooks—even the bands Peace Pype and Love Children are in pursuit. Sheepshead Bay is that kind of place, a thin veneer of hippie peace and love and, just below, a bedrock thuggery and violence.

My most unruly friends, Peter and Blaise, provoke the riot. I'm still in line trying to get past the bouncers when it happens: A wave of furious heaving, swearing, punching from heavily cologned punks breaks over me, dumping me on the sidewalk on Emmons Avenue. I scramble to my feet. The first guy who charges me is five five, skinny, not looking to cover himself in glory. I swat him away and duck into Joe Bo's idling Pontiac—just another Friday night. From the back seat, I watch Pots aspirating blood on the glass, and I wonder, what will it take to get a normal life?

Sheepshead Bay is not Kansas. We're nephews, cousins, and *goombardiele* (godsons) of fearsome individuals: Junior, Gerry Lang, Andrew Mush, McIntosh, all grew up or hung out on the canal. They're my parents' childhood friends. I park their Caddies in Monte's lot on Sunday afternoons. Hollywood has this one piece of wiseguy lore right: Anyone under the mantle of a family is untouchable without enough diplomatic back-and-forth to confound Henry Kissinger.

Word goes out. The disco bouncer works in private sanitation, a wiseguy domain. Now *he's* in trouble. Honey advises us to let it go, and we do, though I can't get the image of Pots's bloody face out of my mind. He's always been a hard-luck guy.

✦ ✦ ✦

In the mid-1960s, Vietnam seeps into Gowanus like a poisoned tide, on television, in the tabloids (*Daily News* columnist Dick Young churns out nonstop rabid pro-war screeds). Vietnam is debated by the gin rummy players in the Glory Social Club, by gamblers who couldn't find Asia on a map; if they could, they'd bet on it. Even the Goose, our loan shark, is a political hawk. Gold stars twinkle in the windows of row houses. Safe at school thanks to a student deferment, I dread my friends getting wasted, and one does—Joe Marcantonio, whose sister Anna has every boy in Gowanus moonstruck.

Pots is still working the nightshift at the pie factory.

Eight percent of the twenty-seven million men eligible for the Vietnam-era draft are inducted into the army. Gowanus, where shirking responsibility is a high art, gets an even lighter dusting. Pots has no tickets to punch; he's unmarried with no parental or child-support obligations, no college deferment, not even a respectable criminal record. He doesn't play the conscientious objector card or scour Manhattan armories for National Guard and reserve units that will never be deployed. He simply hangs around waiting for the draft board missive, which always begins with "Greeting."

When I appear for my physical at Fort Hamilton, half a dozen guys are wearing dresses, shins dripping blood from last-minute razor hacks. They are rejected.

Pots is notified he's 1-A.

✦ ✦ ✦

Gowanus is big families, small apartments, ramshackle row houses, a guest room an unimagined extravagance. So it's a waiting game to see who will invite homeless Dennis Pots home on weekends. There aren't many takers. One Friday, we're standing around sipping warm beer by the mailbox on Carroll and Third, watching cars full of young people returning from a night in the City. The conversation—all he talks about are cars—has petered out, and I can read the hangdog look on his face: another night in the back seat of a junk car parked in a dry cleaner's lot on President Street.

"Come with me," I tell him. "But you gotta be quiet!"

He grins and nods his head awkwardly like he's doing his Frankenstein character. He doesn't understand a real monster lurks at my house, hopefully asleep.

✦ ✦ ✦

"Jekyll and Hyde" is too subtle for Joe Coppola, a man who accelerates from calm to towering rage in an instant, whose shouts and imprecations shake the house, who slaps my mother and smashes the lamps and cheap furniture she's so proud of, who kicks and punches my brothers and me senseless, who insults me a thousand ways but never teaches me how to swing a baseball bat or field a ground ball, who curses the living and dead at the top of his lungs using vulgarities that shame me to this day.

Years later, I stand at the entrance to a civil defense bomb shelter, trees crashing all around me, as the leading edge of Hurricane Frederic devastates Mobile, Alabama. Next morning, I marvel at the purity and perfect calm of the day. A metaphor for my home life.

Yet, with his scant earnings, my father buys his four sons Barricini Valentine's Day hearts until we are teens; he spends endless hours in an apron in our tiny kitchen preparing holiday feasts—antipasti, ravioli, lasagna, stuffed calamari, baked clams, lobster sauces, stuffed veal breast, roast chicken, artichokes, and half a dozen other dishes so delicate and nuanced that I still can't re-create them with my fancy knives and designer cookware. On the worst day of my life—my wife runs off with our infant son—I'm in my bedroom sobbing when Joe, debilitated by emphysema, literally crawls up the stairs to comfort me. When my teenage cousin develops lymphoma—his parents are living in Miami—Joe drives the boy to Memorial Sloan Kettering Cancer Center in his beat-up Cadillac twice a week for a year. He'll do the same for his son Thomas.

✦ ✦ ✦

Pots and I stumble through the front door, making too much noise. Crowded into the tiny vestibule, I turn the knob of the hollow wooden door that opens into the parlor, forgetting the string of tiny Christmas bells that serves as a doorbell.

Loud as Big Ben.

"Fuck!" I hiss.

I grab his arm and hurry past the wooden bathroom door. A plastic Russian *Madonna and Child* icon covers the splintered hole my father punched halfway through. Pots doesn't notice it or the chandelier, my mother's most beloved possession, a gift from her cousins the Pepes. The acoustic tile ceiling dictates it hangs five feet above the linoleum floor. I'm six feet tall and stare down at it every time I walk in.

On the pitch-dark staircase, a do-it-yourself job, stumbling up the uneven steps, I laugh, the scene is too ridiculous. Then we're both giggling. At the landing, I push Pots into my bedroom, pull the door shut, and duck into the bathroom.

A minute later, I hear the tiniest creak on the stairs, a footfall.

"Shit!!"

I'm nineteen years old, in college, a decent kid, so why don't I step into the hallway, toothbrush in hand, and explain to Dad, now halfway up the stairs, Garrison belt coiled in his hand, that Pots has nowhere to go and I've offered him shelter? Granted, it's not Joseph and Mary arriving in Bethlehem on Christmas Eve, but it's the right thing.

A year before, Joe rescued me from two 78th Precinct cops who were beating me senseless with nightsticks on the steps of Our Lady of Peace, the parish church where I was baptized and made my First Communion. My brother Thomas happened to be walking by, saw what was unfolding, and ran home to our father. I was guilty of nothing more than annoying the nuns in their convent with rocks.

Minutes later, 190 pounds of pure rage comes hurtling across Third Avenue, dodging trucks and the B37 bus, blowing past the gamblers clustered in front of Tony's Barbershop and up Carroll Street.

"The fuck away from my son!"

By the time the cops recover, an angry knot of Italians has gathered in front of the church. Hardly sympathetic to Irish cops—everyone knows they're on the take—beating up neighborhood boys.

"He just called me 'son,'" I think goofily. So moved by his words, I don't notice the rage purpling Joe's face is directed at me.

"Stupid bastard!" he shouts. "Embarrass our family in front of the whole neighborhood!"

"Da . . ."

"You embarrass me?"

"Da!"

Now he's punching me. The cops stand back smirking, and I break free and dive into the back seat of the patrol car, where a thoroughly battered Ernie is sitting.

"I hate you!" I scream through the wire grating.

Joe is arguing with the cops, demanding they let me go.

"I'm staying here!" I shout through my tears. "I'd rather be in jail!"

✦ ✦ ✦

Pots is in my bedroom. In the bathroom, I decide to wait for the storm to pass. In an oft-practiced motion, I brace my back against the bathroom door, extend my legs to the edge of the bathtub, and lock my knees. He'd need a battering ram to smash the door open.

"HOW MANY FUCKING TIMES HAVE I TOLD YOU . . ."

A belt hisses in the air. Once, twice . . .

A scream. A double scream. Pots, hiding in the dark under the thin coverlet on my bed, is yelping in fear and pain, my father in astonishment when he turns on the light and discovers he's beating someone else's kid.

He stomps back into the hallway, throws his shoulder against the bathroom door, but it's half-hearted. My mother and three brothers are all awake.

"Joe, what are you doing!" Gloria pleads.

He retreats down the stairs to his living room lair.

⟡ ⟡ ⟡

I'm a college junior when Pots is drafted. I've got a new girlfriend, the second in my life. I'm driving a truck for a commercial laundry run by Herbert Pearl, a hot-tempered man with a bad heart. Inevitably, I begin to pull away from Gowanus. My close friends and family are spinning precipitously into drugs and disaster. Others work dead-end jobs on Wall Street or in the few factories still employing working-class whites. Others, with connections, become entry-level wiseguys now sporting razored haircuts and silk suits on the same streets we'd played stickball as kids.

Fat Ernie, of all people, becomes a corrections officer in the New York State prison system. He's promoted to captain. Later, he confides he's had to sear the eyebrows off a few troublesome inmates to maintain discipline. He's sure I understand.

Pots reports for basic training. Months later, he's discharged, seemingly for spending broiling days at Fort Benning in Columbus, Georgia, feeding a barrack's potbellied stove until its tin roof glows. Later, when I'm teaching at a vocational high school, I'm astonished to learn Pots is running a garment factory. He's engaged to the owner's daughter. I attend his wedding.

I've worried about Pots as long as I've known him. You'd think I can rest easy, but I'm no different from anyone who grew up in Gowanus. I worry as I write these words.

Pots, of course, gets divorced.

Another lifetime later, he's remarried and living in Tennessee. I vaguely recall his mother being Southern, so I convince myself Pots has inherited a big farm or sprawling tracts of timberland handed down for generations. Oddly enough, Ernie, too, is living in Georgia, his daughter a nurse at Emory University Hospital. Now I visualize Pots as a country gentleman sipping Tennessee whiskey on the wide porch of a plantation. Ernie and I drive one hundred–odd miles through beautiful countryside to visit, only to discover Pots is living in a very modest apartment packed to the rafters with his new wife's trinkets and souvenirs, next door to a fried chicken shack.

Pots does have two Corvettes in his driveway, but both have seen better days. The blond surfer's locks have given way to a bushy mountain man beard. Grossly overweight, he tells us he has a bad heart. Also, he's dying. I talk him down from that—he's seemingly misunderstood his doctors' words—and of course, he wants to talk about Corvettes.

At one point, his wife, a sweet woman, appears holding a set of clean sheets and insists we sleep in their bed. When it's time to leave, Pots hands each of us a beautiful Buck knife.

"I love you guys," he gasps.

Over the next five years, I have a medical crisis of my own. I can't make the drive into Tennessee. Pots becomes a disembodied voice on my phone. I can hear the loneliness that's been there his whole life. The heart condition is real.

It kills him in the spring of 2024.

CHAPTER TWENTY-FOUR

The Race

Overnight, the Beatles drive doo-wop into a ditch. West Coast culture seeps into Gowanus with the Beach Boys and Jan and Dean. "Dead Man's Curve," "409," "I Get Around," "Surfin' Safari" blast on our car radios, bewildered wiseguys notwithstanding.

Let's go surfin' now
Everybody's learnin' how . . .

"Da fuck is surfing?" Mikey Bats demands from his perch outside Tony's Barbershop.

The Rolling Stones are en route, and Vietnam's just a shot away; it's a world on the cusp. Aching to be a part of things, I've swapped personas like other boys trade baseball cards—patrol boy, Boy Scout, coin collector, rock collector, fisherman, thief. Nothing sticks until a passing interest in cars as vehicles of escape, travel, and seduction metastasizes into obsession. My cousin Matty D'Alessio takes me around in his '59 Cadillac Eldorado convertible, a chrome-dripping leviathan, eighteen feet long with Flash Gordon fins and a front bumper lifted from a B-52 bomber.

Now I walk Gowanus, memorizing makes, models, years, engines, and horsepower and test myself like it's the college boards. To my astonishment, a Lamborghini Miura, among the rarest sports cars on earth, is often parked outside a grimy Third Avenue storefront. No one dares approach it. There's a seagoing Amphicar across the street from my house, propellers tucked under the rear bumper.

My friend Peter's bronze Caddy and Johnny DiMucci's yellow Electra convertible are now deemed instantly lame. Johnny enters the police academy and moves on. Toupee-wearing Peter, his self-image inseparable from his car, deconstructs.

On 86th Street, between Bensonhurst and Bay Ridge, is Mitchell's Drive-In, only five miles but light-years from Gowanus where dinosaurs—Cadillacs, Chryslers, Lincolns, Electras—rule the earth. Mitchell's is West Coast Kar Kulture in Brooklyn: Corvettes and Mustangs, street rods painted candy-apple red and tangerine orange with exposed chrome-dripping engines, phallic shifters, throbbing exhausts, carhops sashaying in the headlights like strippers.

Good vibrations? Hardly. Drivers are hitters, rowdy Irish and Italians from Coney Island, Bay Ridge, and Bensonhurst; junkyard-prowling Jews from the Flatlands; leather-jacketed Poles escaped from McCarren Park in

Greenpoint, bulked up on steroids, oozing attitude like grease in their ducktail haircuts. (In Gowanus, quarter-inch razored hair and gold chains are the rage.)

✦ ✦ ✦

Mitchell's is a world I recognize from "Little Deuce Coupe" and Jan and Dean's dark anthem "Dead Man's Curve." Subtract the sand and quavering harmonies, and you're in a no-man's-land—insanely dangerous, outrageously illegal street racing.

> *Dead Man's Curve, it's no place to play . . .*
> *Won't come back from Dead Man's Curve.*

Cross Bay Boulevard and what's called the "Connecting Highway" in Astoria, Queens, are Le Mans and the Indy 500, but First Avenue behind the Bush Terminal warehouse complex in Sunset Park is just five minutes from my house. Late one night (practically the first line in "Dead Man's Curve"), four of us, a clown car, arrive in Joey Barbella's Rambler. We watch thundering muscle cars race along deserted piers lit by eerie amber-orange sodium lights, cheered on by a stoned and drunken mob. Big money changes hands, arguments erupt, smoldering adolescent sex mingles with exhaust fumes and burning rubber. I look for the girl in the yellow Corvette, *If you beat me, you can eat me* stenciled on her rear bumper. People still talk about her.

When the crowd thins, Flagman, a *borracho* ("drunk") from the tenements under the Gowanus Expressway, windmills his arms, and Barbella faces off against Joey Formisano's VW bug. I'm in the Rambler; its putt-putting engine sounds like air escaping from a penny balloon.

Bumper to bumper, we pass the steel stanchion, marking the quarter-mile finish line.

Barbella doesn't brake; he rocks back and forth willing the Rambler forward. Blue-eyed and pompadoured—his grandfather owns the neighborhood funeral parlor—Barbella fancies himself Brooklyn's Elvis, an Elvis who can't sing or even twitch. In Gowanus, of course, he's nicknamed "Corpse." Comb in pocket, collar upturned, he drags me to lame Presley movies, plays "Are You Lonesome Tonight?" on the top floor of the funeral home while mourners sob in the chapels below, gets me mugged by Black Apaches in a half-empty Fulton Street theater, *Blue Hawaii* flickering on the screen.

He doesn't brake.

The strip ends in a sweeping left turn onto 39th Street. Fifty-five miles per hour is too fast for an overloaded skinny-tired sedan. I feel the two outside wheels lift—we're gonna flip—when Barbella relents, and we crash sideways through a chain-link fence and down an embankment and come to a stop astride a railroad track.

No third rail, no ruptured gas tank, my face not shredded by splintering glass. Joey Formisano stumbles down the embankment to reach us. Strikingly homely and highly sensitive—the *nonnas* cackle, "*Nemmeno ad un cane!*" (Not even to a dog!) behind his back. In our guttural dialect, it sounds like "monkey-gog."

"Play dead!" I whisper.

Staring at our inert bodies, Joey drops to his knees.

We pop up jeering.

✦ ✦ ✦

An automotive arms race breaks out: Barbella now drives a new Mustang, courtesy of his grandfather, record player under the dash. Honey buys Ernie a silver Plymouth GTX he manages to wreck as he leaves the dealership. Joey Formisano, whose immigrant father owns a fish store in Bed–Stuy, drives a Grand Prix; Lenny, a fuel-injected Corvette. Working two jobs, I can't raise four hundred dollars for a '53 Ford hot rod kept atop a gas station lift, so out of reach, it might be on a Roman obelisk. I have to wait until I'm thirty to buy my four-hundred-dollar car, an Alfa Romeo. I still have it.

Lenny lets Peter drive the new 'Vette. He blows the engine, and laughs. Lenny, broke, is forced to return the car to the Chevy dealer on Fourth Avenue.

We don't slink into Mitchell's now; we strut, particularly when Lena is along. Sixteen and precocious, she lives with her jumpy bandleader father and copper-haired ex-showgirl mother above a candy store by the canal, a trail of boys like ants at her door. Utterly reckless, she tags along when a man so feared, people hesitate to say his name, invites a dozen families to his fifty-acre Catskills estate for a picnic. She bides her time, then slips into a bedroom—everyone is at the pool—and makes off with watches, wallets, jewelry, cash. She heads for Miami. After time passes, all is forgotten. Wiseguys can be oddly forgiving. She's alive today.

At Mitchell's, a guy with slicked-down black hair and elevator heels saunters over. In LA, he might be a lifeguard. In Odessa, Texas, a second-string quarterback.

In Brooklyn, ambitious and overreaching, he's heading for a fall, the never-ending story. The Catalina he drives looks like a family sedan, but it's a marauder with three carburetors and thousands of dollars in performance modifications.

He smirks at the Mustang, lolls his tongue at Lena. In Gowanus, there'd be a fight; at Mitchell's, it's a race.

✦ ✦ ✦

Saturday night. A dozen cars pull out of the drive-in, heading for Highway 278, connecting the Verrazano Bridge, Belt Parkway, and Gowanus Expressway. There's not a cop in sight on a six-lane elevated expressway buzzing with traffic. I'm enthralled as an intricate ballet unfolds around me: cars slow, peel off, and line up side by side, blocking the road. Horns blast; brakes screech; traffic backs up.

Mustang and Pontiac sit idling. A guy strolls between them like it's a Sunday afternoon in the park. Holding a white scarf, he inches the cars forward until front bumpers align. Behind us, more shouts and cursing, a long line of headlights. Mitchell's guys don't give a fuck.

The guy drops his arm. The Catalina roars away. The race takes less than twenty seconds. We lose big-time. In LA, it's a "wipeout."

✦ ✦ ✦

Riding the zeitgeist, the dark-haired guy—the Catalina driver—graduates from drag racing to drug dealing. In 1968, federal agents seize ten pounds of methamphetamine in his car. Sixteen years later, he travels to Corsica and reopens the infamous French Connection drug pipeline. He smuggles six hundred pounds of morphine into Arizona, converts the haul to *three hundred pounds* of heroin, worth twenty-three million dollars on the street. Back in Little Italy, wiseguys take note—not a good thing.

The pipeline springs a leak. In 1986, the smuggler is indicted on dozens of RICO charges. He's caught attempting to flee with an exotic woman and a million dollars in his suitcase. Racing over, he disappears into the federal prison system.

My friend Peter keeps racing against the clock. In a blinding rainstorm, his bronze Cadillac jumps the divider on the Northern State Parkway and rams head-on into a family sedan. I still see the woman's face embedded in the sedan's shattered windshield. Peter lives another ten years. He'll die of a drug overdose.

CHAPTER TWENTY-FIVE

Union Busting for the Mob

Brooklyn College is the last stop on the grim Flatbush Avenue subway. I make the round trip five days a week, sometimes walking an extra mile to the Avenue H station, hoping to see a raven-haired young woman in a fringed suede jacket I'll never have the courage to approach. I assign her names like Meadow and Sage and give her a suitable backstory. I've enrolled at Brooklyn essentially for the $350 Regents Scholarship cash stipend—even in 1965, a beggar's mite. I have to work Christmas and spring break when I watch the campus empty as thousands of students head for Miami and Fort Lauderdale.

I visit Peanuts, the dispatcher at Cambie's Trucking on Third Avenue who hires helpers to unload shipments of Del Monte pineapples and peaches—the sickly-sweet smell of leaking cans first intoxicating, then nauseating—delivered to Long Island warehouses and then to supermarkets. Peanuts operates in a cloud of cigar smoke out of a gray trailer on a garbage-strewn lot next to *The Jewish Press*, a windowless, soulless monolith, once an MTA power-generating station, literally around the corner from my house. Built by the city at enormous cost but never used, its valuable copper cable stripped and sold pennies on the pound to local junkyards. Peanuts is not around, and Cambie's front office is run by an irascible dwarf. I have no prospects there.

I peer through the plate glass window of Monte's Venetian Room, a Brooklyn landmark. Though directly across from my house, I've never eaten there, not counting meatball sandwiches Red the Chef sells out the back door. Monte's is the haunt of the powerful Brooklyn political boss James Mangano, feuding Gallo and Colombo wiseguys, and slippery lawyers from Borough Hall who take lunch meetings in the back. Nick Montemarano, who grew up on the canal (hence "Venetian Room"), is a visionary who'll transform sleepy Gurney's Inn on Montauk Point into a jet-set destination, one of those immigrant quantum leaps that actually happen. His granddaughter Ann Marie will marry Robert Trump.

In Monte's, waitresses have names like Baby Doll, breasts like melons, hair like tagliatelle. I've seen blond Joey Heatherton—Long Island's answer to Ann-Margret—squealing in the arms of diminutive Uncle Honey, who carries her shrieking across Carroll Street and tosses her into his backyard pool, her long dancer's legs fully exposed. Another night, I fight furiously for a fistful of coins Tony Bennett scatters on the sidewalk.

No sign of Honey. I cross Carroll, walk down a narrow alley lined with plaster gnomes and dwarfs to the side entrance of his house. I'm hoping he'll have Peanuts hire me as a laborer at forty dollars a day. I'm tall, husky, awkward, rarely without a book. The door is open—no one would dare rob Honey—and I step in expecting the usual shouted "*Mammone!*" The Scandinavian housekeeper does not appear. (Bay Ridge has a huge Norwegian population.) Normally, a very high stakes poker game is underway at the kitchen table.

Unannounced, I walk into the living room.

Honey is sitting next to Gennaro "Gerry Lang" Langella and a hulking black-haired Irishman named Hugh McIntosh, nicknamed "Apples" by the tabloids, though I can't imagine who would dare say such a word to his face. They stare coldly at me. These are men—I've seen it—who will beat you to a pulp or worse for looking the wrong way or saying the wrong thing.

Honey breaks the silence. "College boy, what is it?"

"I'm looking to work," I blurt. "I thought maybe Cambie's . . ."

"He's a college boy," Honey explains to excuse my lack of respect for arriving unannounced. "Joey Coppola's son."

I allow myself to breathe.

Gerry Lang, handsome and beautifully dressed, briefly worked with my father at the Black Diamond Lines pier in Red Hook. A year or so before, my friends and I had "voluntarily" moved a truckload of his furniture from one Brooklyn apartment to another.

"You wanna work?" Gerry asks.

"Yeah, sure."

What I want is to get the fuck out of there.

"Be here tomorrow. Seven a.m. Got it?"

"Yeah . . . Yes!"

"What are you waiting for?" McIntosh, big as a bear, growls.

There it is. A job to die for?

✦ ✦ ✦

Six thirty a.m. Gloria fixes me soft-boiled eggs and toast for breakfast on my first day on a new job. My father, already en route to the docks, would kill me if he found out what his college son was up to. As I'm leaving, I stuff something preposterous—*Moby-Dick* or *Troilus and Criseyde*—into my back pocket. A knot of men is gathered in front of Monte's, smoking, sipping coffee from plastic cups. Wiry, jumpy guys looking dangerous or stupid. Wannabes from outside the neighborhood, low-level thugs looking to make a day's pay, settle a gambling debt, or impress a wiseguy. They flick their cigarettes and stare with suspicion at me with my walrus mustache and long hair.

I know I won't be unloading cases of pineapple juice. I've drawn an ethical line in my head about how much criminality I'll be willing to engage in for forty dollars, though I haven't considered how to keep that line in front of me. I decide moving stolen merchandise around New York City is an acceptable risk.

This is a world before *The Godfather* exalted organized crime and romanticized violence. To me, gangsters are adults who encourage you to drink, smoke, watch dirty movies, who give you the keys to their new Caddies and Lincolns, not giving a shit if you have a driver's license. They drink, gamble, fight, hang out with celebrities, flash thick wads of money and flashier women. They shoot off gigantic firework displays on July Fourth and suggest we build enormous bonfires in the middle of the street on Election Day, sometimes burning up all the phone lines in the neighborhood. They join us throwing eggs at responding firefighters.

Our parish pastor Father Mario Ciampi can often be found drinking in Monte's or the Capri Club with wiseguys. I watch cops from the 78th Precinct use patrol cars to taxi gangsters from Third Avenue to the Nestor Club on Fifth and Carroll, next to the funeral parlor. I've seen cops walk out stuffing brown paper bags of money into their uniform blouses.

In short, I'm naive or way ahead of life's curve.

Forty-five minutes later, McIntosh drives up. The grim, hulking figure from the night before is gone. This Apples is manic, jocular, dressed in a double-breasted blue blazer and a yachting cap with gold braid on the visor. No one questions this fashion statement.

He circles his finger like we're on *Rawhide.* Everyone piles into half a dozen cars parked in front of Monte's.

"Mustache," he says. "Ride with me."

The caravan moves along Third Avenue to Atlantic, turns left past the shuttered Ex-Lax factory and the first bloom of yuppie antique shops elbowing the Sahadi Brothers and other venerable Arab trading companies that perfume the air with nutmeg, turmeric, and cardamom, past the bleak ten-story Brooklyn House of Detention, and onto Cadman Plaza and the Brooklyn Bridge. I sit folded like a ventriloquist's dummy in the back seat while McIntosh goes on giddily about banging cocktail waitresses—I know one of them. He's a rock star, rapt audience hanging on to every word.

I have no idea where we're going or what we're doing, but I'm not willing play Starbuck to this Ahab. We bump off the FDR near the Willis Avenue Bridge, the crumbled Bronx as unknowable as the moon to me, and into a shabby truck rental operation. McIntosh gets out, stretches, and pulls a wad of bills from his pants pocket. The three cars behind us nose into parking spots. A deal for four straight jobs (medium-size trucks) is arranged. No paper changes hands; no one asks to see driver's licenses. We divide into pairs—driver and helper.

"You, ride with me." A slight, sallow-faced driver who resembles John Cazale taps my shoulder. I figure I'll be doing the heavy lifting. That's fine. I'm walking to his truck when another guy, rugged-looking (think James Caan), about my size, says, "The kid's with me."

The first driver backs off, shooting me a dirty look. I open the passenger door, its hinges shrieking, and climb aboard. Toss my book on the seat. I don't know my driver's name, and he never asks mine.

Twenty minutes later, we're rumbling behind McIntosh's big sedan, bumping up, down, and across Bruckner Boulevard, the Grand Concourse, Morris Avenue, lost.

It's eleven a.m. on a day that threatens to go on forever. Many pay phone calls later, we pull up at our destination, a manufacturer of metal office furniture. I relax. I can muscle desks and chairs all day long. Through the truck's grimy windshield, I notice a crowd of Puerto Rican men and women milling in front of the factory. To me, New York is an overlay of races and ethnicities, all of them alien.

What I do recognize is a picket line.

My father is a laborer, a member of the International Longshoremen's Association, a die-hard union man who'll spend thirty-five years in the vermin-infested holds of ships so my brothers and I can attend college. McIntosh gets out. The union pickets with their sad cardboard placards look at him nervously; he's as big as a pro wrestler. Ignoring them, he swaggers up to a white guy wearing a shirt and tie, one of the factory owners. A brief and heated discussion ensues. The terms of the deal are changing. The white guy, clearly unsettled, hands a roll of bills to McIntosh, who counts it and stuffs the money into his pocket. He nods, and the retractable steel gates of the shipping dock shriek to life.

Doffing his yachting cap, McIntosh strolls up to my door. "Fuck these Jews!" he says.

I reach for the door handle. "What do you need me to do?" I ask my driver.

"You don't do nothing. They do it!"

One by one, the forklifts come out and load our trucks.

I can't bear to look at the men on the picket line.

An hour later, we leave, trucks fully loaded, and drive maybe via the Cross Bronx Expressway—I don't recall and wouldn't recognize it—to a much larger facility, a tan brick warehouse surrounded by tall chain-link fencing. As we approach, my driver flicks away his cigarette and rolls up his window.

"Make sure it's locked."

"What?"

"The fuckin' door! That's what!"

I look up. A much larger picket line, maybe forty strikers, is blocking the gate to the warehouse. A couple of the pickets are pointing at our trucks, shouting. Someone has alerted them. Two NYPD squad cars are angle-parked, bubble gum machines flashing, against the curb. A beefy, red-faced sergeant and a couple of patrol guys are yelling and shoving, trying to restrain a suddenly angry mob.

My guilt is instantly transformed to fear, queasy and visceral. My door won't lock. The push-button latch mechanism is gone. I stare at the sad little hole where the button should be.

"Here!" The driver throws me a length of clothesline.

Where did he get that? I wonder.

"Tie it!"

To do that, I have to lower the window, which barely cranks, and anchor it to . . . what? I remember two knots—square knot and sheet bend—from my Boy Scout days.

"Tie the fucking thing!"

I fumble around, wrapping the rope around the pillar of the vent window.

"Throw it over here!"

He grabs for it, pulls the rope taut, wraps it around his door handle, all the while driving and eyeballing the pickets. Then he pulls a short length of pipe wrapped in electrical tape seemingly out of the air, lays it across his lap. I have a paperback.

At that moment, McIntosh's car glides in front of us. He gets out, casual as a lord, and strolls over to an unmarked police car—I've completely missed it—parked across from the pickets. A police lieutenant, tall, Irish-looking—in these days, most cops are—gets out. In full view of the union men, the two begin to chat like old friends, soon laughing and smirking. They step out of my line of vision. I don't see what happens after that.

Despite the *GQ* blazer and preposterous yachting cap, or maybe *because* of it, McIntosh cuts a fearsome figure. In Brooklyn terms, he don't "give a fuck!" Not for the law, for cops, for unions or factory owners, for fashion, for himself.

According to newspaper stories I later track down, he wears a size-52 suit, carries an ice pick, drives himself to the hospital after being shot in the groin, half strangles the rogue Mob boss Joey Gallo, and especially doesn't give a fuck for society. Years later, he'll die a terrible death, broken and sick in prison, as will Langella.

He certainly won't give a fuck for me, but looking back, I suspect that as a "college boy" from a rough neighborhood, I trigger a certain curiosity in the man—think a bug pinned to a piece of Styrofoam.

How rough is Gowanus? Years later, armed with an Ivy League degree and working for *Newsweek*, I stop by with my colleagues at a bar on the corner of Madison and 49th, the Dallas Cowboy. The conversation is often dominated by well-known columnist Pete Axthelm and sportswriter Peter Bonventre. The bartender fawns over them and ignores me. My buddy Dave Friendly and I are usually too stressed out from writing what seem to be impossibly difficult stories to notice we're being snubbed.

One day, glancing at my name on a credit card, the bored bartender asks where I'm from. "Third Avenue and Carroll Street, near Monte's." He asks a few questions. I mention unmentionable names. From that moment on, whenever I walk in, he finds a way to announce proudly, "Vince is from the roughest neighborhood in the city!" So rough, it's nonstop crime and violence for one hundred years. Even the undertakers tried to kill one another.

✦ ✦ ✦

The police lieutenant gives a signal, and the unmarked car drives off. The patrol cars leave. It's us—the Mob—against the union. McIntosh and a couple of his boys stride up to the gate. Hand in his blazer pocket, he stares hard at the protest leader and says, no doubt, something terrible. The man hesitates; his face crumbles; he backs off. The picket line collapses, and we roar through. Of all those men, only one, a *borracho,* has the courage to step forward and curse us in Spanish. His friends drag him away.

There it is. Jewish factory owners hiring Italian gangsters, using Irish cops to break the poor. It is the end of my love affair with the Mob.

Inside, our truck is offloaded by scabs driving forklifts. As we wait for the rest of our convoy to come through, I sit by myself on a pile of cardboard and try to read. I can't focus. When I look up, McIntosh is standing over me.

A book is a curious thing.

"Mustache!" he says after a moment. "You like this kind of work?" I have the odd sensation that my answer matters to him.

"Yes. I do. Thanks."

He peels off a wad of bills and hands it to me. I shove the money into my pocket. Later when I check, it's two hundred dollars.

"See you tomorrow bright and early!" he chirps and walks away, yachting cap perched on his massive head.

Next morning, my mother, a fearless woman, walks down Carroll Street to Honey's house.

"My Vinny is sick," she says, standing in the doorway as the drivers and helpers begin to gather outside Monte's.

"He ain't working today."

CHAPTER TWENTY-SIX

Bruno and the Dwarf

In a dank, pipe-dripping garage on Columbia Street, Bruno Rubeo and I are bolting an oven into the beat-up truck he's bought at a Jersey auction, his latest, greatest nonsensical scheme. Bruno, who graduated from film school in Rome, emigrated to New York—where we meet—and skidded from advertising to high-end design to painting to sketching twenty-dollar watercolors on the Brooklyn Promenade and now to pizza making in a converted US Postal Service truck.

"What are yous doing?"

From under the propane tank, I look up at a pair of tiny, buckled loafers, miniature gray sharkskin slacks, a black leather jacket that would fit my ten-year-old brother, topped by an enormous head.

"Fuck!" I think. "Armando the Dwarf!"

Yes, Armando Illiano, a four-foot-tall wiseguy, a member of the Gallo gang who compensates for height with towering attitude and occasional spectacle. Armando runs numbers and helps Palmina, his widowed, black-clad mother, look after Gallo headquarters, a ramshackle tenement and social club around the corner at 51 President Street, upper floors fitted with mattresses for the brushfire wars fought against Junior Persico and the Colombos.

Then there's Armando's other job: He walks and feeds Cleo, the lioness Crazy Joe Gallo keeps in the President Street cellar. In the jungle, this concrete jungle, the lion guarantees that men who run afoul of Gallo's loansharking, gambling, extortion, and other predations don't sleep tonight, or any night.

A dwarf walking a lion on a Brooklyn street on a Sunday morning as church bells sing is bound to attract a modicum of attention. When I drive across the Gowanus Canal to pick up cannoli and *pasticcio* at Cioffi's for our family's afternoon dinner, I often see Armando and his outsize shadow swaggering along Columbia Street. Once, he shoots me a murderous look for daring not to stop as he saunters across the deserted street. Cleo is not around.

"I said, what are yous doing over dere?"

"Making a pizza truck," Bruno answers innocently, his florid Roman accent startling Armando. This is decades before food trucks appear in New York. "I'm gonna sell pizza at the soccer games in Red Hook Stadium."

Bruno Rubeo is brilliant, enthusiastic, and naive, a hypercreative artist who transforms the dreary thirty-eight-dollar-a-month apartment above the garage into a live-in movie set with shiny orange floors, tables that convert into beds, yellow sofas that double as storage units, and sculptures and red fabric wall hangings everywhere. Son of a Roman postal worker and a doting mother whose recipes he spends decades trying to re-create, he has an outsize interest in women and Transcendental Meditation and somehow loves the Italian pop band I Pooh (as in Winnie-the-Pooh) *and* the Grateful Dead. When his sister, Gianna, his only sibling, visits New York, he slips her a tab of mescaline and takes her directly to a Dead concert.

◆ ◆ ◆

"Yous can't do that," Armando says.

"No, I figured it out," Bruno says. "This oven cooks at four hundred and fifty degrees. I'm gonna make the dough upstairs." He nods at the garage's sagging ceiling. (The owner has offered to sell him the whole building for four thousand dollars, a price he can't afford.)

"Are yous deaf!"

I scramble from under the truck. I'm two feet taller than Armando, but the guy gives off menace, the perfect avatar for Gallo's murderously absurd family, the *Gang That Couldn't Shoot Straight* journalist Jimmy Breslin calls them. With the rest of the crew, Illiano is dragged into the 76th Precinct on Union Street to stand in lineups, should a victim fail to recognize a four-foot-tall perpetrator. His cousin Frank "Punchy" Illiano is also part of the Gallo crew, as is my Carroll Street neighbor Louie the Syrian, who's shot by a rooftop sniper as he stands eating a pushcart hot dog on Columbia and President.

In a world where deformity is often treated as high comedy, Armando is willing to wear dresses and lipstick at Halloween parties. He makes a show of peeping under real girls' dresses in the social club, a routine the Gallos and the girls apparently find hilarious. He carries a gun.

"Yous gotta pay me first!" says Armando.

"Pay you?" says Bruno, blinking.

"To do business!"

In the 1970s, there's an influx of young craftsmen, carpenters, artists, painters, and sculptors in Gowanus's abandoned lofts, factories, and warehouses. A group of cabinetmakers move into 457 Carroll Street, a space abandoned by Golten Marine. After decades of desolation, I'm elated to see new blood and the stirrings of economic life, but a new generation of wiseguys shakes down these kids, drives them off.

Bruno looks at me, perplexed. "What's he talking about?"

"Don't be a fucking wise guy!" Armando glares at Bruno. "I get tree hundred dollars a month starting Saturday."

He flicks his cigarette at the full propane tank next to me and stomps off.

Bruno never pays Armando. He does sell pizza in Red Hook but never more than a few. A year later, in 1972, Joe Gallo is murdered on his birthday at Umberto's Clam House on Mulberry Street, leaving the dwarf *de-capo-tated.* Bruno retrofits the pizza truck into a camper and swaps fetid Gowanus for the pristine Delaware Water Gap. He prepares his mother's spaghetti carbonara in the woods. Then he gets an idea to ship a Ford Galaxie to Rome, where he's convinced himself there's a huge untapped market for cheap, outsize American cars. There isn't. Gasoline is six dollars a gallon in Italy (versus thirty-seven cents in New York City), and the Ford is too ungainly to even negotiate many Italian streets. When I visit Bruno in Rome, a chorus of blaring horns and shouted imprecations greet us everywhere we turn. When we stop by to visit Mama Sylvana, she's hung my photo on the living room wall. I'm inordinately proud.

In 1973, Bruno moves to Toronto to paint full-time and avoid the IRS (he's declared Luna, a Dalmatian, his daughter). Soon after, he puts together a hugely successful show—one of his paintings acquired by the National Gallery of Canada—crowded with the rich and fashionable. I'm the hatcheck boy trying to keep track of a room crowded with sexy girls in furs. But he never hesitates to take the next risk or make life-altering choices. A year later, he films a documentary on the Trinidad Carnival; it's never screened because of red tape. Next, he designs a computer graphics machine, an early Chyron, but his Canadian partners make off with the patent. He winds up trading paintings for groceries in the Italian market across from his loft.

The next time I visit Toronto, Bruno is sprawled in a director's chair at a public access TV station, filming a group of Eastern European folk singers who can't speak or understand two words of English—or Italian.

"Camera one!" he shouts. "Camera one!"

They turn to camera two.

In the mid-seventies, Carlo Rambaldi, Bruno's mentor at Cinecittà studios in Rome, moves to Hollywood. A special effects genius, he wins *three* Academy Awards (*E.T.*, *Alien*, and *King Kong*) in six years. With a boost from Rambaldi, who's fixated on obese women and needs a wingman, Bruno gets a job designing worms for *Dune*, the sci-fi classic based on a book he's never read. After *Dune*, his career explodes, his quirky personality no small part. A guy who hoped to sell pizza in Red Hook leapfrogs from Armando the Dwarf to Arnold Schwarzenegger and Danny DeVito (*Conan the Barbarian, Twins*). He designs

Salvador, Platoon, Talk Radio, and *Born on the Fourth of July* for Oliver Stone, and a dozen other films. In Mexico, he meets, and the next day proposes to, Mayes Castillero, a talented and beautiful young costume designer so determined she smuggled sneakers across the border to make a few extra bucks. Suddenly, Bruno has a sprawling Mexican family. He's nominated for an Academy Award for *Driving Miss Daisy,* becomes Taylor Hackford's designer of choice.

That funky Gowanus walk-up on Columbia Street gives way to a palazzo, Cent Amore (One Hundred Loves), once owned by a Napoleon niece in Trevi, an Umbrian hill town rising from a sea of olive groves. Trevi is so small its medieval ghetto is one house. Of course, Bruno can't be still. He installs electronic shutters and a digital watering system for his window flower boxes. In this fairy tale palace, Sylvana makes me *polpette* and spaghetti *all'Amatriciana.* Bruno flies her to Hollywood for the Academy Awards.

✦ ✦ ✦

With success, Bruno never loses his enthusiasm, never stops searching for *la ultima.* When I visit Trevi, he loads his car with plastic jugs and drives miles into the countryside to show me the source of *la ultima* spring water (a rusty pipe). An ancient farmer has *la ultima* tomato seeds, traceable, Bruno says, back hundreds of years. We visit a tiny trattoria overhanging a mountain stream for *la ultima cinghiale* pasta. A hairy wild boar carcass hangs in the kitchen in testimony.

Bruno hosts Oliver Stone, Richard Gere, Cindy Crawford, Helen Mirren, Giancarlo Giannini, and Taylor Hackford, who make the pilgrimage to his palazzo. Jimmy

Santiago Baca, a brilliant Apache-Mexican poet who leaps from prison to Allen Ginsberg's poetry chair at Yale, is a regular at the pool of Bruno's Sherman Oaks house. Of course, they're served Sylvana's carbonara. An artist creates an indelible caricature—*The Pasta Police*—depicting him as Mao Zedong in uniform and red star cap, demanding "your best dish!"

He ships an enormous Buddha from Shanghai to Trevi. Townspeople crowd the square to marvel at the spectacle. In Umbria, Bruno is now *il regista,* the director. He designs an underground parking garage trying to help attract tourists to the sleepy town. (Booming Spoleto is fifteen minutes away.) Bruno delves ever more deeply into Traditional Chinese Medicine, acupuncture, tai chi, Eastern philosophy. In 2008, when Suzanne and I visit at Christmas, I bring bottles of Chinaco, *la ultima* tequila. He lectures me—I'm all for cutting-edge science—about yin and yang; opposing energies; earth, wind, and fire; happiness and sadness.

He treats what turns out to be aggressive prostate cancer with herbs and potions, then delays until the tumors burst outside the capsule. Only then does he turn to Western medicine. I'm so furious.

I speak at his Hollywood funeral. Helen Mirren follows.

In 2019, Mayes Rubeo Castillero, Bruno's widow, is nominated for an Academy Award in costume design for *Jojo Rabbit.*

We stay in touch.

CHAPTER TWENTY-SEVEN

My Cousin Richie

I fly to New York with my children for my kid brother's wedding. He's booked one of those glittery Bensonhurst palaces Italian Americans so love, a seventeen-piece orchestra, Lucullan feast, plus *cocktail* hour, *Venetian* hour, mountains of elaborate desserts and rivers of liqueurs, *midnight* hour, dozens of waiters laboring under trays of eggs Benedict, bacon, sausage, waffles, pancakes, pastries, and a cornucopia of fruit. My new sister-in-law has rented a tuxedo for my four-year-old son and a stylist for my twelve-year-old daughter.

A family wedding with hundreds of guests. There's a wiseguy table stocked with Armani-clad men and their mink-wrapped wives and girlfriends right next to the kiddie table. My wedding unfolded in a justice of the peace's wood-paneled basement in Yonkers, *Here Comes Da Judge* displayed on his desk. My brother Joe never showed up—he was playing football in Red Hook—but lent me his blue leather platform shoes with red soles and his clear plastic belt. Thomas, who did attend, provided the geometric polyester shirt and a red-striped regimental tie. My white pants and a blue blazer a dollop of understatement.

Unknown to me, the groom just quit the IT job I moved mountains to secure for him at *Newsweek*. I'd convinced myself it would provide security, a sense of being part of the larger world, things that matter to me. He wants to be a bookie draped in an Italian suit with cash stuffed in his pockets. His dream is as unrealistic as mine. He's awash in gambling debts and has drained his pension; the clock is ticking.

✦ ✦ ✦

Bensonhurst. When we arrive in our limo, my female cousins are screaming.

"He's coming! He's coming!"

"Who?"

"He's starring in a movie with Robert De Niro!"

"Who?"

"What are you, a fuckin' owl?"

That from my cousin Carol.

"Richie! Richie Castellano!"

Richard Castellano who played portly Clemenza in *The Godfather* ("Leave the gun, take the cannoli") died ten years ago. One shrieking teen from New Jersey thrusts a headshot in my face. It's autographed "Richard Castellano," but the smiling, broken-nosed visage is my cousin Richie, aka Richie Mel.

Everyone knows that.

✦ ✦ ✦

The next time I saw Richie was on Fifth Street in Park Slope. I was trying to teach English lit to auto mechanics in Williamsburg. That morning, half asleep, I'm unlocking my Karmann Ghia when a hoarse shout jolts me.

"Cuz! You gotta help me!"

"Hey, Richie. What's up?"

"Cuz! I'm begging ya!"

Everyone from Gowanus shouts. All day, all the time, as if they're players fretting and strutting on some invisible stage. The rest of the world is scenery for them to chew.

"What's wrong?"

"Cuz, they say I robbed a gas station!"

"What?"

"I'm innocent. I swear to my mother! They saying I shot a guy—with a shotgun!"

"Get outta here!"

"Fuckin' cops! You know how they lie!"

I did know.

Ten years before, I'd made the mistake of getting drunk on Tango, cheap vodka and Tang. It was a school night when I was swept up in a dragnet—there'd been a street gang murder—and dragged into the 78th Precinct. A cop pummeled me for hours trying to force a confession.

Richie pauses as if to find his mark. "Cuz, you're an educated guy. You went to college. I'm stupid! You gotta help me! I know I did some bad things, but I'm innocent this time. I got a wife."

He sniffles. "Maybe . . . maybe you could talk to Uncle Sonny."

Our uncle Sal Giordano is an NYPD sergeant so straight, he's known in the neighborhood as "Eliot Ness."

"Uncle Sonny knows people."

"I could call him."

Uncle Sonny's impulse would be to strangle Richie. For years, he and his wayward brothers, JuJu, Jimmy Psycho, and Popeye Anthony, have been the bane of Sonny's existence.

"You could write a letter to the prosecutor," Richie adds hopefully. "I'm thinking the bishop too. My sister Carol works in Our Lady of Peace Rectory. She cooks for the priests. Cuz, I'm really scared."

"What's his name?"

"Who?"

"The bishop."

"Fuck I know!"

I'd always felt Richie and his brothers—all smart, engaging, personable guys—were a photographic negative of my own family, victims of some mysterious affliction, the curse of growing up on the Gowanus Canal. I and two of my brothers are college grads. None of us has ever been in serious trouble (this would change). I feel guilty. I've committed the sin of hard work and ambition.

"I'm fucking innocent!" he sobs.

"Come on. It's okay."

I give him a pretend hug. "Nothing's going to happen. I promise. When I get home, come by. We'll eat. I'll help you. Okay?"

This is the Vietnam era, the Watergate era, the Berrigan brothers . . . Injustice, civil rights—he's hooked me.

"You mean it, cuz?"

"Sure. But I really gotta get to work now."

"No problem. I don't want to bother you. I know you're a busy guy. Responsibilities."

As I'm tossing my briefcase stuffed with papers I've spent hours marking into the Karmann Ghia, Richie calls out again.

"Cuz?"

I sigh and stand back up. The tears are gone. He's grinning. I stare as he pulls a greasy wad of bills from his pants pocket. Hundreds of dollars. He fans it in front of my face.

"Cuz," he says. "But I got the money!"

He can't resist. He has to let me know I'm an idiot.

✦ ✦ ✦

Years pass before I see Richie again. Released from jail on the robbery and other felonies, he's now a prizefighter. Our family has a pugilistic history. One of my earliest memories is a newspaper photo of my maternal grandfather, club fighter Jim Jordan, standing, thick arms raised in triumph over a battered Black man, Stonewall Allen, the Fighting Parson, at the Pelican Athletic Club in Bay Ridge in 1906. The caption: *Prayers did not help him.*

All seven Jordan (Giordano) brothers were outsize men. Two were pro wrestlers in the 1930s, one supposedly a Russian. In Chicago, according to family legend, a fan sitting ringside hears this Russian hiss in Neapolitan—"Take it easy! Goddamn it! You're hurting me!"—and the jig is up. Grandfather Jordan had hopes for his eldest son, but my uncle Tony's nickname ("Punchy") said it all. Richie represents a third generation of family fighters.

He's holding court in Snooky's Pub on Seventh Avenue, surrounded by a knot of intrigued women—I'm reminded of De Niro playing Johnny Boy in *Mean Streets*—the same girls, braless and casually available, whom I, with my droopy mustache and faded jeans, my teaching job, my books, and bullshit, cannot get close to. This is post-hippie Park Slope. The communes of the sixties when a brownstone on Polhemus Place cost sixty thousand dollars (if you could find a lender) are passing away, replaced by yuppies pushing Peg Perego prams who believe no one and nothing of value existed before they arrived.

Trim, blond hair cut unfashionably short, nose suitably broken, Richie spots me at the front of the bar.

"What is it? Cousin Vin! Get over here!"

Here we go.

"This is my cousin. He's a schoolteacher."

Instantly, the women's eyes glaze over. With a ninth-grade education and fourth-grade grammar, Richie spent two years working on his prison memoirs in longhand, on spiral tablets in multicolored ink. They arrived at my apartment every few months.

"Cuz," he'd suggest on one of the many collect calls I'd accept, "polish this up a little. You know how. We split the money!"

After wading through a blizzard of misspelling, cliché, and repetition, I don't have the heart to disillusion him when he calls to check on our "investment." Richie is nothing but resilient. To my relief, he's surrendered his literary aspirations with his orange prison jumpsuit.

"Cuz, I'm fighting next week in Sheepshead Bay," he crows, shooting jabs in all directions. "Gonna kill this fuckin' guy! Am I right, ladies?"

The women instantly perk up.

"Cuz, get these girls some drinks. I'll get yous all front-row seats."

The fight is staged at a street festival near Emmons Avenue. Tickets are free. Gulls circle like vultures. Richie is knocked out in the first round, a dying swan, his rebroken nose streaming.

"Cuz, I'm bleeding!"

✦ ✦ ✦

I often fly up from Atlanta to visit Gloria. On clear days, I can pick out the Gowanus Canal and the Williamsburgh Bank as the Delta jet banks and descends into LaGuardia. As a kid, I'd lie in our yard watching those same flights passing overhead, trying to imagine what exotic places they were headed. This time, I'm crossing Third Avenue, the Carroll Street Bridge glimmering in the summer haze.

"Help me, Cousin Vin! They're gonna kill me!"

Richie is clinging to the wrought-iron fence of the apartment building on Third and Carroll. His mother, my aunt Jenny, lives upstairs. An Electra sedan idles at the curb. Two thugs are holding him, trying to pin his arms and drag him into the waiting car. This in broad daylight. I don't know them, but I grew up with the third, Charley, a Colombo family capo standing on the sidewalk. Charley had been a serious, thoughtful young man, never intimidating, always interested in my career as a reporter in the South. Our parents are friends. Charley had the misfortune of being born into a particularly ill-starred and oft-targeted Mafia family.

"Cousin Vin!" Richie shouts frantically.

Fat Rosie and Gowanus's other resident gossipmongers are all watching.

"Vinny," Charley pleads, "would you get this fuckin moron to shut up?"

"They're gonna kill me! Please don't let them take me!"

"Nobody's gonna hurt you!" Charley hisses.

"Richie, it's okay!" I say without thinking.

All I want to do is see my mom. Once again, I'm

caught in his mad web. At any moment, I know Gloria will be out the door charging up the street to rescue her nephew. Charley takes me aside and explains. While in jail, Richie claimed to have juice among the correction officers and administrative staff of a particular prison in Upstate New York. He's so well connected, he insisted, that for a few thousand dollars, he can guarantee that somebody's son, nephew, father, or cousin will be provided exceptional treatment and perks—the best jobs, unfettered access to food parcels, choice of cellmates, books, who knows what. An offer no one can refuse. With wiseguys being incarcerated at a dizzying pace, it's a perfect though wildly reckless scam. This doesn't stop Richie from collecting thousands of dollars, money funneled to a girlfriend at the time—and then disappearing on his release.

Paroled, he can't stay away from Gowanus. Word is out. Another family in Bensonhurst or Howard Beach has put a hit on Richie. Charley patiently explains all this to me as if what I think counts. I don't understand this world or its arcane rules, but my cousin—certainly no made man—is under the protection of a certain Mafia faction. This immunity, a very long story, goes all the way back to his father, Uncle Fat, crippled by a Southern trucker driving through a dockworkers' picket line.

Richie was going to a meet. After which, some guy will "throw him a beating," the phrase suggesting how casual and impersonal the business of violence. Richie will live to scheme another day.

And, of course, he does.

✦ ✦ ✦

When the movie *Analyze This* premiers in 1999, I swear I spot Richie standing alongside the two stars Robert De Niro and Billy Crystal. My brother Joe tells me he's seen him too.

"What the fuck!"

The comedy is about a wiseguy, De Niro, suffering a mental crisis, who drafts a reluctant psychiatrist, Crystal, for help.

I track down Richie's sister Carol, who proclaims him a hot new star. "Richie's got a big part in it," she gushes. "Richie got me on the set! Robert De Niro kissed me!" Translation: "Fuck you, Vinny, and your college education!"

As Jimmy Boots, De Niro's "dese and dose" bodyguard, Richie croaks just sixteen lines ("What are you, some kind of moron?" the most memorable), but like a virus, exposure is more than enough to infect an exponentially bigger—and more naive—population than Italians living along the Gowanus.

In Hollywood, I'd seen throngs of unemployed actors clustered Sunday mornings in Studio City, comparing notes and filching casting calls. Dozens of Italians: New York Italian, Chicago Italian, San Francisco Italian, blue-blood Italians from Rome and Milan; artistic, handsome, beautiful, stupid, charming, effeminate, dangerous, talented Italians (Chazz Palminteri is parking cars), few of them going anywhere.

Here's Richie giving TV interviews, fabricating madly: "I come from a big family with Mob connections . . . When I was a kid, I saw people killed . . . By the time I was twelve or thirteen years old, I was an alcoholic. That was the only life I ever knew, the only thing . . . So I was a street guy, a bank robber (the gas station magically transformed). And in order to survive, one of the skills you got to develop is acting. I been shot, beaten to a pulp with lead pipes, you name it, at various times in my past life—I've even been pronounced DOA one time when they took me to hospital. Altogether, I survived ten contracts on my life."

Ten!

Richie has an agent. He has a website. He's organizing a film festival. He has a French wife!

I don't. This is too much!

✦ ✦ ✦

Richie is no longer another quirky Gowanus character. This Richard Castellano is brand-new news. He and his wife, Marie Jocelyne-Helene Rousseau, who, as it turns out, trails a string of aliases, are living on the Delaware River in Narrowsburg, New York, plotting to rip off the entire populace. This is spring 1999, a few months after *Analyze This.* I know because I've tracked him down.

"Cousin Vin! Where you been!" he shouts over the phone, genuinely excited to hear my voice. There's something irresistible about the guy.

And inevitable.

In a breathy French accent, Jocelyne (a woman of many names) invites me to the first annual Narrowsburg Independent International Film Festival. A thousand miles away, I feel the familiar virus singing in my blood. Surely my cousin Richie will find a place for me at the festival.

Won't he?

✦ ✦ ✦

Richie arrives in Narrowsburg draped in black leather in the back of a black Cadillac. An outsize bodyguard, Armondo "Mondo" Bilancione, is hunched behind the wheel. It doesn't take long to create a stir. On the strength of sixteen spoken lines in *Analyze This,* he opens the Richard Castellano School of Acting. Forty-two townspeople sign up. Sixteen lines and he convinces the burghers of Narrowsburg their hamlet will soon be "the Sundance of the East." A chicken farmer named John Borg paces up and down in a frenzy of anticipation. Sixteen lines and Richie announces he'll be starring in a gangster movie—*Four Deadly Reasons*—to be shot, for some unfathomable reason, in Narrowsburg. Of course, he'll be employing local actors. There may be opportunities for investors.

For a month, Richie struts, lapels flying, down Main Street, shouting at everyone he meets, playfully shoulder punching stolid insurance agents like they're goombahs.

"WHAT IS IT?" he demands.

His life is an open book, only fiction. The gas station he'd confessed to robbing is now an armored car. In court, it will shrink to a shoe store. He has "two million dollars stashed away." He's killed people, danced away from "contracts" on his life. By the Gowanus, these fantasies are dismissed with a knowing grin and a playful slap in the head. In Narrowsburg, they're intoxicating, a dizzy taste of life at the fountain of celebrity.

Mornings, Richie shows up at the Chatterbox Café on Main Street, buying everyone breakfast, then breezing out without paying. He brings in street corner guys from New York City to populate his movie, supplements them with local "talent." Tosses checks to vendors like rice at a wedding. John Borg, the chicken farmer, is cast as a "Marshal Dillon–type character." Borg, who lives in a double-wide trailer, invests $154,000.

Seasons change. Richie's checks float like cherry blossoms, then bury the hamlet in blizzards of red ink. In August 2001, *Four Deadly Reasons,* Richie's star turn, is screened to a packed house in Narrowsburg. He's nowhere around. The rough cut will later be described by Alex Blumberg on *This American Life* (December 15, 2000) as "a porn film without the sex scenes, awkward dialogue, noodly soundtrack, gratuitous use of bikinis and double entendres, and not one scene with people from Narrowsburg."

All attempts to recoup payments for goods and services fail. The townspeople turn to lawyers and law enforcement, real ones. Ultimately, Richie is arrested and charged with four felonies. He's also named a defendant in sixteen civil suits involving rental cars, equipment, meals, and, of course, talent. Among the aggrieved parties: Mondo Bilancione. My cousin gets a restraining order against his own bodyguard. Then his attorney sues him.

The felonies are tied to yet another scam—selling bogus Screen Actors Guild cards to aspiring actors, essentially the same con he'd pulled years before with real wiseguys in Brooklyn. At a preliminary hearing in Sullivan County Court, Richie's histrionics are right out of *A Few Good Men.* He interrupts witnesses, rants, then pleas, then ignores contempt threats. "Richie acts like the judge is a director," remembered one witness.

Ultimately, he plea-bargains, agreeing to restitution and a year in county jail. Richie finally takes responsibility for his misdeeds. Then he *doesn't show up for sentencing.*

I wonder about the sheer stress of being Richie, pinballing from one scheme, one con, one relationship to another, ducking creditors, cops, wiseguys, enemies, and ex-wives, somehow maintaining the image, the confidence, the bluster, the bullshit. Being on all the time, the outsider all the time, must be so exhausting. Even as a kid, crowded above a grocery with a physically and emotionally crippled mother, a father who obeys absolutely *no rules,* and five siblings who even by Gowanus's loose standards are out of control.

After his disappearance, the *Sullivan County Democrat* reports that Richie has been found naked on the Verrazano Bridge attempting suicide. Then he's arrested walking "half-naked" in Manhattan and taken to Bellevue Hospital for psychiatric evaluation. There, he claims he's "taken too many shots to the head as a professional fighter." A cynic might suggest a method to this madness. Next, he's in drug rehab.

Finally, hauled into court in an orange jumpsuit and shackles, Richie asks Judge Frank J. La Buda for a "personal favor." His daughter is getting married on Staten Island.

"Can't you find it in your heart to let me go to my daughter's wedding?"

"This is not *Let's Make a Deal!*" La Buda, who's had more than a year of Richie, snaps.

Outside, John Borg, the farmer who lost his life savings, is holding a hand-lettered sign reading *Hang 'em high!,* a testimony to Hollywood's impact. Some of the funds that dribble into Narrowsburg over the next months to cover

Richie's twelve-thousand-dollar restitution are twenty-dollar money orders, suggesting our family and our old Gowanus neighborhood didn't forsake Richie once his star had dimmed.

✦ ✦ ✦

The seventh "edition" of the Queens International Film Festival kicks off in winter 2009. Its founder and executive director is Jocelyne Castaldo, Richie's French wife. Dogged by creditors and toxic press reports, the festival is, of course, a disaster. Jocelyne's life, a tangle of cons, scams, unpaid creditors, and threatening ex-husbands scattered across three continents, makes Richie seem naive, almost innocent.

Of course, he always was.

We all were.

Oddly, when Jocelyne is finally arrested, it's for animal cruelty: abandoning forty dogs without food or water in a locked feedstore in Kingston, New York. It's still unclear what her intentions were. Convicted of those charges and multiple counts of fraud, she's shipped to Rikers Island—Devil's Island apparently unavailable—and then deported to France.

On his release, Richie returns to New York City, the brash, in-your-face persona I remember now muted. He tries stand-up comedy, auditions for movies, but his five minutes are clearly over. He rekindles a teenage romance with a Gowanus girl named Brenda, who, unlike the women in his imaginary movies, never abandons him.

It's 2015. Saturday night. Over the phone, Richie complains to Brenda about experiencing chest pains. Easter morning, she shows up at his Queens apartment. No answer. The two have plans to spend the day at Brenda's house. Frantic, Brenda calls his son, Richie Jr., who assures her everything is fine, that Richie had gone out Saturday night. She knows this is not true. Two days later, Richie Jr. finds his father unresponsive.

Dead of a heart attack.

CHAPTER TWENTY-EIGHT

The Secret

Barbara never said a word, not even when the medical examiner ruled that Bobby died of natural causes. She was standing outside her house when Ralphie and Raymond beat Bobby senseless, stomping his head again and again against the curb. Annette, who lived right down the street, triggered the rage animating Ralphie. She was Bobby's girl. They'd been together that mild autumn night.

Barbara watched Bobby stagger to his feet and make his way up Carroll Street like it was Calvary Hill. He made it to Fifth Avenue near Scappy's club, where wiseguys and wannabes huddled like extras in some never-ending *On the Waterfront* loop. They did nothing. Bobby was an outsider in our constricted world, a nobody. He stumbled past the Garfield Theater, the gas station, and into the basement of 347 First Street, even then careful not to disturb Louis Pellecchia. The two were estranged for all the reasons that alienate controlling fathers and rebellious sons. Dennis Pots, who lived up the street, remembered

Louis had "a throne in their living room," though Pots was hardly trustworthy.

Bobby woke with a throbbing headache, worse than the migraines he'd suffered for years. Louis, PhD and the Brooklyn Navy Yard's 1961 Engineer of the Year, had already left for work. Bobby's mother, Victoria, was at her chores and never saw him leave. He caught the B63 bus to Lawrence Street, then walked the few blocks to bustling Fulton Street, and into E. J. Korvette's record department. That week, Petula Clark's "Downtown" and the Supremes' "Stop! In the Name of Love" were big with teenyboppers from East Flatbush.

Later, Bobby stumbled into the men's room in such pain that witnesses recalled him slamming his head against the wall. Before police and EMTs arrived, Bobby collapsed and died alone on the restroom floor, the first of my friends to die.

Word spreads in the hours and days that follow. Bobby wasn't from Gowanus, had no extended family to grieve and mourn aloud, offer comfort, or demand vengeance, no shrieking chorus of *maldicenze.*

Ralphie was safe.

✦ ✦ ✦

In 1965, the distance between Gowanus and Park Slope is immeasurable. Bobby is nineteen, a college student whose father earns triple what Joe Coppola brings home. Louis Pellecchia has investments, owns rental properties that will be valued at millions of dollars in the decades ahead. If he misstepped, it was in choosing to live on the border between heaven and hell, a porous boundary.

I don't know a single adult who finished high school. Bobby lives on a tree-lined brownstone street, thick with doctors, near Prospect Park. I live next to a factory with my parents and three brothers, sleep on a convertible sofa. I'm self-conscious and insecure; Bobby picks is cool and confident with a girl, a job, a future. Tall, good-looking, smart, and funny, Bobby picks up girls on Brighton Beach as I stand mute. If he had flaws, I never saw them.

In every community dwells the myth of the exceptional young person—athlete, caregiver, scholar, musician, artist—carried off by cancer, KIA in some faraway land, eviscerated in a car crash, or swept up in inexplicable tragedy. Bobby is that guy. His official cause of death, cerebral aneurysm, is incomprehensible given his youth and vitality.

We all grew up on the same streets in what feels like another world. Only fate set us apart. We all lived under one immutable commandment: "Never talk, never rat, never confide in an outsider." No matter outrage or injustice. Barbara stayed silent until her own children were grown, and her husband, Fishy, my friend and elementary school classmate, was losing a long battle with lymphoma . . . until the Gowanus we knew no longer existed, its laws no longer enforced.

Fifty years passed.

In 2013, I arrive in New York City for a consultation at Mount Sinai Hospital. I've been diagnosed with stage 4 squamous cell carcinoma, endured chemo, radiation, a neck dissection. My future is clouded. The Gowanus is a Superfund site, one of the most polluted waterways *in the*

country. My family lived on the canal for one hundred years. Gloria pushed my baby stroller over the wooden planks of the Carroll Street Bridge above green water that hissed and bubbled like a witch's cauldron. She developed the same cancer I now have, was treated at the same hospital.

Neither of us ever smoked a cigarette.

I visit my old friends, ranks thinned by age, illness, and the burden of being born in such a place. A dozen of them are waiting when Suzanne and I arrive at the Villa Fiorita in Bensonhurst, a restaurant that could easily be Monte's Venetian Room circa 1965. Vinny is our waiter's name.

It's an odd reunion, our memories spool like mimeograph pages, identical until we're in our twenties: no cross-country trips, no Florida spring breaks, no draft dodges, law school, or backpacking in Europe. We lived in a toxic snow globe cut off from the larger world. I'm still swirling in that globe. They see me as the one who got away.

Like Ishmael.

At dinner, Bobby Pellecchia, an apparition from our collective past, appears like Banquo's ghost. I never understood what drew him from his orderly, middle-class life in Park Slope to the inchoate world of the canal, a place I was desperate to escape. In Brooklyn terms, why did he choose Manual Training High School when Brooklyn Tech was a few subway stops away? Why Gowanus over Park Slope where middle-class Irish girls became schoolteachers and the few Jews and Protestants hippies and rebels?

Gowanus existed outside expectations. For me, there was no overachieving father judging my every step, no great teacher or role model or coach inspiring me. I'd always believed Bobby set the example I followed, the bar I pulled myself over. I now suspect he was an illusion, a creation of my imagination like the gangsters I elevated to role models, a hero I desperately needed. Was Bobby simply drawn to the heat of a neighborhood girl?

✦ ✦ ✦

The restaurant table grows quiet. Barbara, the skinny teen of memory, is now a full-figured grandmother. She relives that October night, vivid details pouring from a wound that never healed. Looking around, I expect disbelief and outrage, and then I realize *they've heard this story before.* In the silence that follows, I understand that, like Ishmael, it falls to me to tell the tale.

This takes years. My life is buffeted by turbulence. A son from a short-lived second marriage on whom I've showered much love and attention self-destructs, drops out of college, joins the infantry, is deployed to Iraq, attempts suicide. Wave after wave of illness crashes over me.

✦ ✦ ✦

We leave so little trace in passing through life. Bobby's friends have mostly disappeared. One, Anthony Viola, dies of Hodgkin's lymphoma traceable to Agent Orange. I'd looked forward to reminiscing, as we did long ago on the Typhoon air-conditioner factory stoop across from Our Lady of Peace church. Now Anthony's life and death are compressed into one moment. Pots dies of the very congestive heart disease I'd assured him was treatable. Fat Ernie, a guy I believed indestructible who gained weight during rounds of chemotherapy, dies when his cancer recurs in 2024.

Bobby's parents are long deceased. Victoria died six years after her son's passing. His father lived into his nineties. Gloria, Bobby's older sister, may be deceased, or else vanished in the Brooklyn diaspora over the Verrazano Bridge and into the suburbs. I can't find her.

I search newspapers, census forms, death notices, criminal records, obituaries. And waiting there is Ralphie. He comes back to me, a surly, unsmiling teen in a long leather coat, an apostrophe of dark hair over the center of his forehead, forever on the cusp of violence. "Not one to mess with," a contemporary tells me.

Bobby did, though unknowingly. Ralphie was obsessed with Annette, and Bobby, in the hero myth we all embraced, was not a guy to be cowed. The rest was inevitable. I stare at the surface of Ralphie's life. He married, had children, was convicted of armed robbery, and served time in state prison. He was paroled, developed diabetes, and died painfully at age fifty-three.

Ultimately, I have no eyewitness evidence that Ralphie had any involvement in Bobby's death. Barbara and Annette, both pivotal players in this story, went on to live happy and seemingly full lives. They have children and grandchildren.

They refuse to talk to a ghost from the distant past.

✦ ✦ ✦

Autumn 1965. On a rainy day a few weeks after Bobby's funeral, Dennis Pots is walking up Carroll Street to Fifth Avenue, the same route Bobby had taken. He runs into a distraught Annette, tries to console her, walks her home. A day later, Ralphie and Raymond, who's wielding a baseball bat, confront him. Ralphie demands to know why Dennis was with Annette.

"I know you're going out with her! Don't fuckin' lie!"

CHAPTER TWENTY-NINE

Dark Rooms

Morning sunlight filters into the dim second-floor bedroom, my younger brother's refuge for the last months. The same room three brothers shared, the room where we dreamed our separate dreams. I'd be a writer; Joe, a quarterback; Thomas, an actor. In Gowanus, isolated on the banks of a poisoned canal, our dreams do not carry the tragic weight of hubris; they're laughable.

Thomas lies there immobile, left eye swollen shut, blond hair lank and burned ash gray by toxic medications, his handsome face disfigured by dozens of purple lesions—Kaposi sarcoma, a rare and "indolent" skin cancer that in AIDS patients is invasive and hyperaggressive, so aggressive that I swear new tumors appear on Thomas's arms and legs overnight. Radiation has turned his swollen legs into leather; my hands ache from trying to massage his pain away.

He's refused any further treatment with alpha interferon—the side effects described as having the flu every day of your life—though the experimental drug kept the raging cancer in check for months. Thomas has survived pneumocystis pneumonia only to be ravaged by other "opportunistic" infections. I have a pistol, but I don't have the courage. I'll never have the courage. Gloria, always the strength of our family, won't allow me to change his linens or help him use the bathroom. She's afraid Thomas will infect me and I'll infect my five-year-old daughter in Atlanta. (It's so early in the epidemic even doctors are nervous.) And there's Gloria's fierce maternal instinct. Seeing my mother cradle her dying son is the *Pietà* come alive

An ambulance is en route to take Thomas to Mother Cabrini hospice on East 19th Street in the Manhattan he so loves. I open the curtain.

"Those bitches!" Gloria says in the hoarse whisper that is now her only voice. "They're standing out there just waiting."

It's too much. I jerk the hallway door open and run down the stairs, half tumbling onto Carroll Street. I'm going to strangle them—Phyllis, Millie, Fat Rosie, and some other neighborhood women I can't recall. Then I notice they're all crying. For Thomas. For Gloria. For me.

Someone hugs me, and now I'm sobbing.

The ambulance pulls up.

✦ ✦ ✦

May 1985. Mother Cabrini is the only hospice in New York City willing to admit an AIDS patient. As his ambulance pulls up to our door, Gowanus memories flood over me—hopscotch, Ringolevio, summer nights splashing under the johnny pump, his ducklings and rescue dogs. Thomas is hand-carried in a chair to the idling ambulance.

Across the Brooklyn Bridge, crowds are gathered near the South Street Seaport. Strains of martial music float in the air. New York's Vietnam Veterans Memorial is being dedicated. Our EMTs are veterans and so kind. Thomas emerges from some unfathomable place and says, "Give them a big tip."

My memories of the hospice are unreliable. One night, a trio of musicians appears, plays Baroque sonatas, and disappears without a word. Visitors arrive, embrace him, and leave in tears. A nun, a portly angel, sings to him in Italian. I visit Green-Wood Cemetery and purchase my brother's grave while he still lives. We sit in shifts, knowing and not knowing what we want of him. He's fed powerful pills he can barely swallow. He moans. The moan becomes a persistent hum, to me a scream. On the fifth day, while we're at dinner, he dies.

He was always kind.

✦ ✦ ✦

When Morehead McKim accepts, I'm literally overwhelmed with gratitude. The funeral director tells me he hasn't "seen anyone so ravaged since Vietnam." I still live with that. For three days, crowds of mourners, friends, family members, and so many strangers show up to say goodbye. Thomas is buried in Green-Wood Cemetery on a bright spring morning, hundreds of cherry blossoms floating in the air.

✦ ✦ ✦

Time passes, empty and colorless.

And then he returns. I'm in our sunlit bedroom, but it's no dream. I recognize the burnt-orange suede jacket, collar upturned, that Joey gave him. When we embrace, I feel the muscles rippling in his shoulders, stubble on his cheek. I want to hold him.

"Please, Tom. Please don't leave."

"I've got to go."

CHAPTER THIRTY

Joe Galapo

Joe Galapo struts into my classroom like a favored guest on *The Tonight Show.* Curly-haired, olive-skinned, mischievous, a purveyor of jokes and magic, oblivious to Norman Goldenberg, my irascible principal, sitting in the back of the room, scribbling notes.

"Mr. Coppola!" he announces in a quavering carnival barker's pitch. "Before your eyes, I am to transform eggs into rubber balls!"

He pulls a black velvet cloth, two eggs, and mason jars filled with blue liquid out of his knapsack, places the jars on my desk and flips them open. The stench is immediate, overpowering, like chemicals in a darkroom. A girl in the front row coughs, and instantly, boys on either side pretend to choke. Like a wave retreating from Brighton Beach, students are up and swirling around the diminutive principal, carrying my job prospects out to sea.

Unfazed, Galapo plops eggs into the jars, covers them, and stands back. The principal glares at me, bald pate crimson with rage, and disappears into the corridor. All this happens in two minutes, the lesson plan I've spent hours working on stillborn. A thirteen-year-old has likely cost me the holy grail in New York City public schools, a job in a white, middle-class school, though some small part of me appreciates the shamelessness of this kid.

"Mr. Coppola, watch how they bounce!" Galapo shouts, dropping the eggs on the tile floor.

"Joe."

Too late. Later, I learn he didn't cure the eggs for the recommended forty-eight hours and substituted an acetic acid far more concentrated than the white vinegar called for in his book of tricks.

"Joe!"

I'm standing, broken eggs at my feet, my students' shrieks and hollers disrupting every class on the floor, the bell about to ring, and four more classes to teach.

✦ ✦ ✦

At Seth Low Middle School, Galapo, undaunted, becomes my shadow, always upbeat, eager to tell a story, ask a too-personal question, perform a trick, giggle at his own jokes before the punch line. Seeming both older and younger than his peers, a stranger in the strange land of adolescence, wanting to be part of things but not knowing how.

Joe was born in Egypt at the tail end of a diaspora dating to 1492, when Ferdinand and Isabella expelled Spain's Jews and Muslims. Five hundred years later, forty thousand Sephardic Jews are in Egypt when Israel's lightning victory in the Six-Day War triggers a wave of relentless anti-Semitism. The Galapos flee Cairo for Paris and then Brooklyn.

How does Joe Galapo fit into a world where his

classmates are focused on banana bikes and the Sicilian pizza at Spumoni Gardens?

He works magic.

He convinces me to take a dozen students, including a girl he has a crush on, on an unauthorized trip to Coney Island, a few stops away on the Sea Beach subway but fraught with as many perils as the *Odyssey*. A bright spring day, Nathan's hot dogs, orangeade, paper cones stuffed with crinkly fries, the boardwalk, getting pounded by the g-force of the Cyclone, and the reeling, ear-shattering Himalaya. The kids follow me like I'm the Pied Piper. We talk of silly and serious things, and I sense they listen. For the first time, I feel that I *matter*, that I can make a difference in other lives.

I'm fired at the end of the semester.

This leafy Bensonhurst idyll is an illusion. The white parents and their kids resent the busloads of Black and Puerto Rican children arriving each morning from the Coney Island projects, themselves refugees from Fred Trump's neighborhood busting. One afternoon, I watch a group of older teens walking, too quickly, toward an idling bus. Jumpy, feral wannabe wiseguys lifted from my Gowanus childhood. No dean, teacher, cop, or crossing guard in sight when they attack, throwing rocks, bashing the shatter-proof windows with bats and lengths of pipe. They do this laughing as terrified children turn round and round trying to escape.

"Niggas, go home!"

✦ ✦ ✦

My next assignment is Automotive High School in Greenpoint. *Manhood, Service, Labor, Citizenship,* inscribed above the entrance across from McCarren Park, a splash of green among grimy tenements, crumbling brownstones, factories, and warehouses bounded by an onion-domed Russian Orthodox cathedral. Automotive is a Public Works Administration project, its architect optimistically included half a dozen tennis courts.

When I arrive, I can't help but notice a plaque commemorating students killed in Vietnam, an outsize number for such a small school. Later, I learn one of the guidance counselors has an "arrangement" with army recruiters, shipping hapless, impoverished boys into the meat grinder. I meet Vice Principal Gerald Greenberg, head of academics, or as the sign on his cluttered desk proclaims, *Chairman of the Bored.* My fellow teachers are former mechanics and dress the part: coveralls, rumpled khakis, and ratty sweaters on assembly days. Gerald Greenberg wears beautifully tailored double-breasted suits and regimental ties. He's well spoken, knowledgeable, debonair, sarcastic.

Eight hundred boys and *one girl* commute from all over the city, divided by race and ethnicity and united by the attraction between teenagers and cars. Barbara, a freshman, is short, blond, tough as nails, and assigned to my homeroom. Giggling postpubescent boys mill outside my door like salmon fighting their way upriver to spawn. One is Joe Galapo, a taller, thinner Galapo, sporting a *Saturday Night Fever* haircut and gold chains.

"Mr. Coppola!" he shouts, bursting into my English class.

I'm teaching Shakespeare using Roman Polanski's *Macbeth.* Blood, gore, murder, and a coven of nude witches are great teaching tools. Matty Martino, who wears shades, boots, and a black leather motorcycle jacket in summer, shoots Galapo a look that sends him scuttling out the door. Matty's from Red Hook.

Joe and I sometimes have lunch at the teachers' table, where baked fish and green Jell-O are *spécialités du chef.* He's maturing, gaining confidence, making friends. A bright kid without direction, I don't see him doing oil changes.

In 1940, my father is an Automotive student, the favored son in a matriarchal immigrant family with a pony, twin six-shooters, and cowboy duds. After his seamstress mother's death, he quits school and hangs with other zoot-suited Gowanus boys. He's drafted into the army, becomes a tanker, goes ashore with the marines at Peleliu Island, a catastrophe from which he never recovers. My grandmother is a name on a tombstone. In Automotive's shadowed basement, she comes alive, the permeable wall dividing the living and the dead shatters as her words and spidery signature leap at me from papers I find in a dusty cabinet.

I stay four years. My students are, as I am, naive, curious, wary. I swap overworked *Freedom Road* for books that made a difference in my life, *Catch-22* and *One Flew Over the Cuckoo's Nest.* I take an eleventh-grade class to see newly released *American Graffiti.* Emerging from the subway at Columbus Circle, I take in the distress these fearsome teens trigger in the lunchtime crowds. They see it too.

In that class, Willert Morris, of West Indian descent, will be admitted to Cornell University. Eddie Walls, a redhead from Harlem, leads our ragtag tennis squad to a division championship. He's offered a spot at the Port Washington Tennis Academy, where John McEnroe polished his game. Ever shape-shifting, Joe Galapo now tells me he wants to be a cop.

Automotive's students vote me Teacher of the Year. I celebrate by spending the day with a blond Texan pianist I met on my first-ever trip outside New York—on the French Riveria. She's auditioning for the Juilliard School. Seeing a substitute teacher, my students disappear. Alphonse Presley, a sweet Black kid from the South, wanders across Bedford Avenue into McCarren Park, a no-man's-land. He's mugged, robbed, and stabbed in the heart. He survives, but the shame of it haunts me.

✦ ✦ ✦

Graduation Day 1975. I've spent four years with this class. Played tennis, run sprints, worked on cars. They've made me proud, frustrated, and furious. We've shared our stories. Peter Lewis, from Antigua, plays guitar in my living room. His memories of the racism his family encountered in the United Kingdom become the basis for a proposal at the Columbia University School of Journalism that sends me overseas and changes my life.

I watch as they line up on both sides of the corridor in their caps and gowns, their proud parents, girlfriends, and siblings in their finery walking ahead into the auditorium. The is the last time I will ever see them. I choke up, speechless and embarrassed. Joe Galapo notices, walks up, whispers something I don't register, and gently shoves me. I float across the hall into the arms of Luis Martinez, a burly Cuban who thinks Castro is cool despite his refugee father's rants, and back again into the arms of

Danny, an Italian from Union Street, and then across to Walter from Harlem. I pinball three or four more times, laughing with my graduates. Feeling a love I've never felt before.

✦ ✦ ✦

In 1978, I'm working as a *Newsweek* reporter. Joe Galapo marries a Jewish girl from the Bronx named Helene Amiel. Ever in a hurry, he fathers three sons in his twenties and graduates from the New York City Police Academy. Joe is assigned to a precinct in Coney Island, site of our long-ago field trip, and then as a plainclothes officer to Brooklyn South's narcotics unit. He loves the work, loves the camaraderie of his fellow officers. The job adds a measure of meaning and significance to his life. Like me, meaning is what Joe craves most.

New York is in the grip of a crack epidemic. Street crime is at an all-time high, another legacy of wiseguys who, according to the bullshit myth, don't stoop to street-level drug dealing. In the evening of August 16, 1988, in Sunset Park, a scuffle breaks out as Galapo and his partner, Sgt. William Martin, are frisking a group of men after a suspected drug buy. One of the suspects, Joseph Barker, whirls and slams into Martin, discharging the cocked pistol in the cop's outstretched arm.

The .38 round strikes Joe Galapo in the face.

I see images, a highlight reel of Joe's sweet and uncomplicated life, flash before my eyes when I revisit this tragedy. Rushed to Lutheran Medical Center and then to Bellevue Hospital in Manhattan, Joe dies that evening.

He's just thirty years old.

✦ ✦ ✦

Four thousand police officers attend Joe Galapo's funeral at the Magen David Synagogue. Rudy Giuliani and Mayor Ed Koch are there. This is all just a few blocks from where thirteen-year-old Joe worked his magic at Seth Low Middle School. Magic that sears me to this day. In summer, you can hear the unmistakable shrieks of preschoolers and the hiss of sprinklers in a leafy park on Bedford Avenue in Sheepshead Bay, the Galapo Playground.

CHAPTER THIRTY-ONE

Losing Mom

Looking back, it seems I'd waited my whole life for the call. It came late in the night the Friday after Thanksgiving, my brother Greg telling me our mother had been rushed by ambulance to Methodist Hospital in terrible pain. The backache she'd barely mentioned when I'd called on Thanksgiving Day will turn out to be a tumor mass—squamous cell carcinoma—that had invaded her lungs and swollen her liver twice its normal size.

The call came three days after my forty-third birthday. Like so many baby boomers, I was living a life vastly different from my parents'. Twelve years earlier, my job had carried me to Atlanta. My brothers, my childhood friends, the house I'd grown up in, the streets I'd roamed were a thousand miles away and fading. Memories of Brooklyn outnumbered my real-world experiences.

Gloria had turned sixty-six a few weeks earlier. Since adolescence, I'd been telling myself how lucky I was to have young parents, how I wouldn't have to worry about losing them until my own mortality had begun to weigh upon me, until the needs of my children forced me to relinquish any claim to childhood. Those illusions were shattered in my mid-thirties, when emphysema debilitated my father, transforming a man whose life had been marked by hard work and self-reliance into a frightened, helpless child.

I'd always considered myself responsible for my parents' well-being, bound by traditions that in one generation had gone from being the right thing, the expected thing, the American way, if you will, to some impractical folkway practiced only by recently arrived immigrants.

Looking back, I'd taken no concrete steps to support this notion. Like so many of my generation, I'd avoided talking with my parents about planning for their aging. They were still young, and I was full of myself. I imagined my life full of drama and tempestuousness. Living it was a full-time job. My parents accepted that. They lived through their children. They had four sons to keep them busy. They never left the street they were born on and never cared to. The likelihood of either or both of them moving to Georgia in a crisis was nil. In neither of my unhappy marriages would there have been a place for my folks. Among Italian Americans, extended families are still viable. A nursing home would have been out of the question.

When things began to go wrong—in taking early retirement, my father had neglected to check a clause that would continue pension payments to my mother in the event of his death—I could offer little more than concern and guilt. My feelings were real, but they wouldn't have put food on the table. Death had come early in our extended family. Aunt Dolly, my mother's elder sister, died of breast cancer in her early forties.

Aunt Marguerite, a younger sister, succumbed to cancer in her fifties. "Not three," I'd told myself. "Three sisters couldn't get cancer." I was younger then. Later, shadowed by the ironies and disappointments that mark our passage into adulthood, I knew the clock was ticking for Gloria.

When Thomas, thirty, developed Kaposi sarcoma, he came home to Carroll Street. Gloria tried to save him with home cooking, prayer, and a mother's love. Every day for a year, my father bucked Manhattan traffic in his old Cadillac, a raging bull on a mercy mission: getting his son to Memorial Sloan Kettering Cancer Center for treatment. They barely spoke, the issues were way too complicated, but one morning, I found my father in the backyard shaking his fists at the heavens.

"Why him? Why him!"

✦ ✦ ✦

Joe Coppola died over the telephone. My part played out in a series of long-distance calls. It took five years and as many hospitalizations. I remember nights when he was so scared, Gloria called the fire department for help. And these big, burly men looked after him.

On March 6, my wife, an actress, landed a television commercial. She seemed happy. (A month later, she'd pack up and leave, our marriage over.) We picked up the kids and headed home. The answering machine's red light was flashing angrily, five, six messages.

"Vinny, it's your brother Joey. Daddy just died."

Again and again, each time the voice choked with panic.

"Vinny, Daddy just died! Please call! Vincent, please! Daddy's dead. He's lying on the floor!"

✦ ✦ ✦

"I can't understand what's happening," Gloria says, her voice a morphine haze. "I went shopping last Wednesday. I was fine. I walked all over the Avenue."

"I love you, Mom. I love you so much."

I spent Thanksgiving weekend in Atlanta lost on streets alone, though surrounded by friends who cared for me, beyond the reach of arms that would comfort me. "We all have to go through this," someone whispered. "It's part of life." Even so, in my car, I howled at the injustice, the unfairness of it. I raged. I cried and hated myself for crying; each tear was an acknowledgment that she was dying.

By Monday, I'd decided I was going back to Brooklyn, and I'd stay however long it took. This was my personal choice, and I attach no moral certitude to it. Everyone makes their own. My boss told me to do what I had to do. "We'll worry about it later." After eight weeks, he fired me.

This woman had given me life, had made my well-being her life's work. She'd sung to me as a child. In our toughest times, seeing me shamed by cardboard stuffed inside my worn-out sneakers, she'd risked my father's wrath to buy me new ones. She still cooked my favorite dishes, still pressed money on me when I was broke. She loved her sons and grandchildren more than herself. The bond between us was fierce. I'd never, as I'd promised, taken her to Florida, Los Angeles, or the Vatican. Never become rich or famous, never danced with her at my wedding. She never cared. Last autumn, swept by some strange prescience, I'd taken six weeks off from work and traveled to New York to write, sleep in my old room, and be her son again. Now would be my time to comfort her and stand with her. This would be the last time in this life I would ever be a son, the child of a living person.

"If God wants me, I'm not afraid," Gloria always told us. "Whatever God wants . . ." I never saw her without her rosary. She supported a stream of church-related charities with five-dollar donations yet could curse a blue streak and hold grudges and always wanted the latest gossip. She attended services three times a week at Our Lady of Peace, one of the last devoted churchgoers in what had been a thriving parish. As a child, it had been my job to stir the gravy on Sunday mornings during the hour she was at Mass. She always sat in the same pew—"Gloria's row," her friends called it. Over the last few years, I'd begun attending Mass with her whenever I was in town. She always wore high heels to church. Young women marveled at my mother's figure. In the three years since her first operation, she'd lost forty pounds and suffered disfiguring scars. She complained she looked "like a skeleton." Still, she wore those high heels. Awash in memories in the nearly empty old church, I'd look at her, and tears would flow. She'd pretend not to notice.

Once, returning to Gowanus was a joy. This time it was a rite of passage. I had come as a son seeking his mother and found myself in an empty memory-haunted house, the head of a family heading for disaster. Greg, who had been supporting Mom since my father's death, was unemployed. Joe was in rehab. Bills were piled up; the mortgage and property taxes hadn't been paid. My parents had managed family finances out of an old shoebox in which they kept payment books and canceled checks. Mom's hospital costs were already in the tens of thousands of dollars and surging. Though well insured, she still owed thousands from her previous surgeries.

Our resources essentially consisted of her small savings account, a two-thousand-dollar life insurance policy, and the modest row house we'd grown up in. Determined to keep the house and our family intact, I worried about losing both.

At the hospital, Mom was being maintained on heavy doses of morphine and little else. We asked that the dosage be cut back and discovered the pain had diminished. Other problems had developed, her feet and ankles had begun to swell with fluid, she couldn't swallow without choking. Her only sustenance was an intravenous solution dripping slowly into her arms. Every day, untouched containers of soup, pasta, fruit, toast, eggs, Jell-O, and tea lined her windowsill. After ten days, she was transferred to Methodist Hospital's third-floor cancer ward for chemotherapy. Each day, I'd imagine the runaway cells inexorably growing, approaching critical mass.

"Do you think this can really help me?" she asked.

"Please, Mom," I said, "there's nothing else we can do."

I'd half convinced myself the harmless-looking liquids in the clear plastic bags above her bed could work some miracle. They were powerful cytotoxins that would kill any fast-growing cells in her body, but she would lose her hair, develop sores in her mouth and the lining of her stomach, experience nausea or worse. On Friday night, she was given a cocktail of painkillers and anti-nausea drugs to prepare her for her first treatment.

I arrived early Saturday morning carrying coffee and a newspaper, eager for some hopeful sign. A nurse stopped me outside the room to ask whether Mrs. Coppola should be revived if she went into cardiac arrest. I rushed past her to find Mom gasping for breath. A nurse was suctioning her throat with a vacuum device. Anti-nausea drugs had suppressed the gag reflex that allowed her to clear phlegm. She was drowning in front of my eyes. We stared silently at each other. Half a dozen other patients were in distress; the nurse passed the vacuum tube and saline solution to me and left.

In the cancer ward, some patients sleep constantly, others never. One woman, suffering from both lymphoma and Alzheimer's, shrieks through the night. Many smoke constantly. One of Mom's roommates, a woman without family or friends, endures three days of chemotherapy and then is supposed to make her way home alone. Gloria orders me to drive her. She has Greg give fifty dollars to another, indigent patient. Despite the high-tech medicine and competent caregivers, the ward is not a place to inspire hope.

On Seventh Avenue, shops are ablaze with lights and decorations. Men hawk Christmas trees on the sidewalk; carols play over tinny speakers. Our house, always bright and filled with people, is dark and empty. Greg and I stay with Gloria in shifts. Relatives visit regularly, but we keep the haunted hours. Other families keep similar vigils; many of the "children" are my age. Two brothers, both in their forties, flew up from Florida at Thanksgiving to visit their mother. A month later, they're still there "trying to get Mom home for Christmas." At the other end of the scale is the daughter berating her dying mother for the "trouble and expense" she's causing. That woman's last months would be spent shuttling between the cancer ward and a nursing home.

Three days before Christmas, I ask permission to return to Atlanta to spend time with my children. Gloria insists I go.

"I'm okay. I've got plenty of company."

Holidays are important in our family; Gloria is passing the tradition to me. As I'm leaving for the airport, torn between my responsibilities as both father and son, she hands me money for gifts and Christmas cards for Gaby and Thomas. Inside, she's written, *Grandma will love you always.*

A patient dies on Christmas Eve. Three days after Christmas, a surgeon cuts into my mother's abdomen, attempting to install a feeding tube directly into her stomach. He fails. Her liver is so enlarged with tumor, he can't find her stomach. A tiny tube he attaches to her small intestine pulls free and Mom refuses to have it reinstalled. On New Year's Day, a forty-three-year-old woman whose husband and daughters have kept a lonely vigil in the room across from us dies of brain cancer. Their wails echo through the ward.

At noon on Saturday, January 5, Gloria is discharged. While Mom was hospitalized, Greg had her dingy bedroom redone all sunshine and bright colors. I'd dumped the worn-out bedroom and living room suites, bought new sofas and a bed—charged it all—framed and hung pictures of Thomas and the grandchildren alongside her photograph of Pope Paul VI. My mother spent her entire adult life living in that run-down house.

On the sidewalk outside the hospital, she can't walk four steps to the car without gasping. The painful swelling that had begun in her feet has bloated her legs. When I massage them, imprints of my fingers remain in her flesh. She can't weigh more than ninety pounds. Her face is gray, her lips pulling back from her teeth.

"It's so beautiful," she whispers as Greg carries her into the house. "So beautiful."

A neighbor prepares lentil soup and runs it through

a blender. She can't eat. At the hospital, she'd ordered Cousin Millie to eat the food I'd bring "so Vincent won't worry." She spends the day exhausted on a BarcaLounger we borrowed from a neighbor.

Sunday night, Greg carries Mom upstairs to her bedroom, the stairway as insurmountable to her as Mount Everest. It takes six pillows to put her at ease, and still she can't sleep. She calls to me in the middle of the night. I lie awake next door in the narrow room that had been mine as a teenager.

"Vincent, my back . . . I can't get comfortable."

I adjust her pillows for the fifth time.

"I'm not letting you sleep," she says. "I made you come up here so far from the kids."

I cling to the iron rail of her new bed. An enormous chasm stretches between the living and the dying, a gap love cannot bridge. I want to hurl myself across it. "Mom," I say, "there's nowhere else in the world I want to be." I realize that I've been granted a precious moment. A chance to say those special things we feel for those we love but so rarely do. A chance to say goodbye.

"Mom, I want you to know that you've been the best mother any son could have. I want you to know that whatever is good and special in me has come from you."

She lies there, staring.

I'm blinded by tears. "Mom, I can't change this. I can't change what's happening to you. You know I would if I could."

"I know," she whispers. "I know."

Monday morning, her blood pressure continues to drop.

"Vincent," she says, "I don't feel good. Maybe I should go back to the hospital."

I don't want her to die surrounded by gaping strangers in a crowded emergency room or wind up lifeless on a respirator. "Okay, Mom. Let's wait a little bit." I know what choice I'm making. The hospital has an arrangement for bypassing admitting procedures on the cancer ward. After a while, it becomes too much. Greg decides to drive to the hospital to find the head nurse. I'm upstairs when Cousin Millie shrieks, "Vinny, come down! Something's happening!"

Mom had pitched forward in the chair. She'd grabbed Millie's hand. She's not breathing. I pinch her nostrils and begin breathing into her mouth. It's the first time I've ever kissed my mother on the lips.

"Breathe, Mom. Please, Mom, breathe! Don't die!" Somehow, she hears me and delays her passing. She comes back but only for a moment. Her last breath passes into my mouth. Later, Josie Stuto, our octogenarian neighbor, will tell me this is a gift.

When I look up, Greg is kneeling beside me, sobbing. "I won't cry," he'd said, "until there's no hope." Millie dials 911. Half a dozen police officers and EMTs pile through our front door, pushing us aside. Mom lies on her back, her pajama top open as a team works to defibrillate her, her ribs and collar bones protruding. It's the only time I've ever seen her undressed. At that moment, Joey walks in. He never gets his chance to say a last goodbye, make amends, and tell her he loves her. Of course, Gloria knew that.

When I write this, the tulips and irises I planted in the yard that last fall are beginning to blossom. I was going to surprise Gloria with them. Her favorite outfits and a few pieces of jewelry are given to family and friends. The rest donated to the poor.

Sometimes, I wonder about the road ahead. I remember the poisonous green tides flooding the cellar, my uncles wading into the noisome water to clear the drains. I remember wiseguys dumping medical waste into the canal. It was cheaper for their corporate customers than loading the toxic material on a barge and ferrying it out to sea, the deals no doubt done in Monte's. As a boy, I played on half-sunken barges, climbed a mountain of metal barrels filled with industrial chemicals. I held magic turquoise crystals and golden powders in my hands. And now there's magic all around me: enormous apartment towers soar on the canal banks, community gardens blossom where sewage flowed, millennials kayak on the Gowanus.

I wish Gloria could see it.

CHAPTER THIRTY-TWO

Under a Full Moon

Old men doze under flat-brimmed caps. *Nonnas* stir Sunday tomato sauce and pull strings of dried chilis from backyard clotheslines. My grandfather puffs malodorous De Nobili cigars and sips Mr. Stuto's homemade wine. A naked light bulb tells us Rosina is frying ten-cent calzones in her cauldron. Pilgrims, we stream to her.

Easter mornings, Chitty lines the sidewalk with potted lilies, offerings we bring after church to our immigrant relatives in Green-Wood Cemetery who occupy some middle world between the living and the dead. Clad in mourning black, women bake Easter pies, heavy *Rustica* stuffed with ricotta, prosciutto, salami, mozzarella and Parmigiano, and delicate *pizza di grano.* I'm crazy for *grano,* a sweet concocted of wheat berries, sugar, butter, eggs, lemon peel, and candied citron. *Grano* is not something you'd find on supermarket shelves. Sold by bakers in brown paper bags, the grain must soak for days.

After Mass, Baby Doll Stuto, Millie Pepe, and Maggie

Christiano appear at our door. They present Gloria a tiny *pizza di grano* wrapped in crinkly aluminum foil.

"Buona Pasqua!"

So delicious and rare.

Bakeries and pastry stores dot Gowanus. The aromas of baking bread, ricotta cream, marzipan, and almond paste perfume the air outside Monteleone's, Court Pastry, and Cioffi's on Union Street, where, rumor has it, Sinatra gets cannoli and *sfogliatella.* Frank is associated with a dozen restaurants, bakeries, pizzerias. He's everywhere, blasting on jukeboxes, on autographed photos in restaurants, wiseguy social clubs, barbershop walls. I've never seen him.

Once a year, Cioffi's bakes trays of *zeppole di San Giuseppe.* My father is Joseph, so on March 19, our many relatives are obligated to gift him boxes of *zeppole,* oval pastries topped with custard, a sour cherry, and powdered sugar. I gorge on them for weeks. But to me, Cioffi's *pizza di grano* tastes commercial, as if baked and shoved out on the counter without love or respect. Over the years, I'll hunt for *pizza di grano* in Rome, Naples, and Palermo, determined to find what my Roman friend Bruno Rubeo calls "*l'ultimo.*" Nothing compares with the old ladies' long-ago creation. When I return to Brooklyn, Gloria always has a sliver of *pizza di grano* set aside, no small thing with my three brothers.

"Mom, just get the recipe," I say, grumbling and picking at the crumbs.

"They won't give it to me."

"What?"

"I've asked them. They won't give it to me."

"Who?"

"Never mind."

"Mom!"

Gloria dies in 1988. My father is already gone; I'm the eldest, head of a disintegrating family. At Gloria's funeral, I stare at her open casket, trying to understand how things had gone so wrong so fast. An old woman hobbles up to me. I kiss her dry cheek, smell old lady perfume. She presses an envelope into my hand. *La busta* (the envelope), a traditional offering of money to help defray funeral expenses, a holdover from our immigrant days. I stuff the envelope into my jacket pocket and forget about it.

Weeks later, I find it. Open it. Written in spidery Italian script, is the recipe for *pizza di grano.* The first line begins:

Under a full moon, soak the grain . . .

I never bake my own.

Acknowledgments

Time was, Gloria, Joe, Joey, Thomas, Greg, and I lived on the Gowanus Canal surrounded by grandparents, uncles, aunts, thirty-odd first cousins, and dozens of other working-class Italian families. A church, a parochial school, three grocers, a butcher shop, a bakery, a social club, two bookie joints, Monte's on Carroll, and Smiley's pushcart hot dogs on President—my world until I was seventeen and left for Brooklyn College (returning by subway every night). I loved my close-knit, raucous community, but didn't realize how deeply, or how many others loved it, until I tried to capture it a lifetime later.

So I thank Aric Press and Jerry Adler, former *Newsweek* colleagues, for bringing what was a collection of social media posts to the attention of the incredibly talented and incomparably decent Sarah Crichton, then editor in chief at Henry Holt. Ironically, Sarah was at the forefront of the wave of "yuppie outsiders" who'd transform Gowanus, Cobble Hill, Carroll Gardens, and

Red Hook (where my father worked "down the docks") forever. Any retroactive resentment dissipated when Sarah asked me to translate a word she'd heard from the Italian grocers selling hero sandwiches on Court Street—"gabagool." Same for Andrew Miller, Holt publisher and president, who apparently grew up ducking Italian punks—my kid brothers' friends—lurking in Carroll Park. Thanks to Meryl Levavi for finding mapmaker extraordinaire Laura Maestro. Also at Holt, my thanks to Stephen Altobelli and Marinda Valenti, who assure me my Gowanus tales will resonate among a new generation of Italian Americans.

Thanks to my agents, Peter and Amy Bernstein, and Mike Ruby for bringing us together.

Never-ending gratitude to Suzanne Pruitt, a Savannahian, who took on the Sisyphean task of reading, critiquing, editing, and easing my doubts over the last twenty years. And to Joe Enright, my classmate at Saint Augustine Diocesan High School, who spent many months researching and fact-checking my stories. There'd be no book without you two guys. Much less a book without my Columbia J-School classmate Mario Tedeschini-Lalli, a Roman who took on the ignoble job of translating the guttural scraps of Neapolitan and Sicilian slang and appalling vulgarities I remembered from my childhood.

Cousins Louise Abatemarco, Ann Marie D'Onofrio-Lucey, Lorraine Garrison, Anthony Giordano, Carole Jordan Binder, and Patty Siconolfi fleshed out family stories where my memory was lacking. Steve Kabacinski, your photographs bring the stories to life.

Abracci to Robert Corum, Dick Friedman, Jerry Grillo, Drew Jubera, Tom Junod, Terry McDonell, Doug Monroe, Kevin Sack, Vern Smith, and Chris Wohlwend, scribblers all, who faced the challenge of bringing long-buried experiences and painful emotions to life.

To Lou Arcangeli, Charlie Augello, Pete Bagley, Zulal Biner, Ezra Cantor, Betsy Carter, Joe Casale, Stanley Chernicoff, Gerry Cooney, Nancy Cooper, Gaby Coppola, Joe Coppola, Frank Cox, Mickey Cuomo, Mike Dowling, Barbara Eve, Bobby and Elisa Ezor, Mary Farmer, Seth Fried, Bob Gaddi, Peter Goldman, George Hackett, Andy Jassin, Nitza Kakoseos, Donald Kaplan, Stephen King, John Kowalczyk, Eliot Mackle, Joey Mason, John McDonagh, DeAnne and Alan Mitchell, Michael Moriarity, Butchie Mulia, Roz Pontone Musacchia, Peter Nasca, Arthur Nash, Barbara Overson Nash, Frank Nemzer, Kate Nerone, Frank Newcomer, Sharon O'Connell, David and Katerine Phillips, Dan and Jane Pruitt, Kay and Dennis Regan, Mayes Rubeo, Lucy Scalici, Jay Smith, Joel Sokolov, Lucian Truscott IV, Bob Wallace, Dan Weinert, your encouragement kept me going.

Grazie tante to the scores of folk from the Gowanus diaspora who returned to reminisce, remind, correct, relive: Anthony Angioletti, Anthony Cataldi, Lou DePalma, Rose Di Terese, John Esposito, Antoinette Froncillo Loggia, Umberto Gallo, Louie Hubela, Anthony Manzo, Mary Rose Manzo Baffi, Nicholas Matteo, Joe Mongiello, John Padovano, Lenny Weyerbacher. You took me back to the Glory Social Club, John's Candy Store, the Capri Club, Our Lady of Peace School's toxic lunchroom. No greater compliment than Emily DelDuca telling me, "Your stories have given me back my life."

And the inimitable "Uncle Honey" Christiano who moved to South Florida in his eighties and married a young Russian divorcée.

I'm heartbroken that Joey Barbella, Ernie Benevento,

Joey Formisano, Frank Garofalo, Peter Lauro, and Dennis Pots are not here to share our stories . . . and that Terry Kay, a writer sprung from the cotton fields of Royston, Georgia, who took the time to read and praise a collection of tales centered on a Brooklyn canal, is gone.

Illustration Credits

Coppola Sisters: Carmine and Rosanna Siconolfi

Coppola Family: Carmine and Rosanna Siconolfi

Coppola Cousins: Carmine and Rosanna Siconolfi

Giordano Family: Giordano (Jordan) Family

Plumbing the American Dream: Giordano–Jordan Family

Gowanus Rising: Joseph Enright

On the Docks: Anthony Giordano

De-Capo-Tated: *New York City Gangland* by Arthur Nash

Partners in Crime: Waterfront Commission of New York Harbor

Garfield Boys at the 78th Precinct: New York *Daily News* / newspapers .com. Photographer: Gary Kagan

All My Trials: *Sullivan County Democrat*

On the Town, Al Fresco, Joe Coppola, Pompadours and Skinny Ties, Paradise Park, Boys' Night at Coney Island, Gowanus's Last Gasp, Thomas Coppola: author

About the Author

Vincent Coppola is the author of five nonfiction books. A former *Newsweek* reporter, Coppola has written feature stories for *Talk*, *Esquire*, *Rolling Stone*, *Men's Journal*, *Worth*, and *Atlanta* magazines. Coppola's story of his mother's battle against cancer was awarded the William Allen White Gold Medal for Writing by the University of Kansas. He is a 1977 honors graduate of the Columbia University Graduate School of Journalism.

Carroll St. Bridge culverts
Gowanus Canal
Hare Krishnas on Henry St.
Wigwam bar
Rooster in front of Goldies on 3rd Ave.
Hare Krishna House
Ferdinando's Focacceria
Armando the Dwarf walking Cleo along Columbia St.
Gallo Gang Headquarters
Monte's Venetian Room
See inset
Kayak on the Gowanus
pigeons
Manhattan Bridge
Brooklyn Bridge
East River
Buttermilk Channel
Governors Island
Atlantic Basin
Red Hook
Flatbush Avenue
Fulton Street
Brooklyn Queens Expwy
Cadman Plaza
Montague St.
Remsen St.
Joralemon
Atlantic Ave.
Gowanus Hamilton Ave. Expwy
Scale in Miles 0 1/2 1 Approximately